THE MA
EARLY AND M

THE MAKING OF EARLY AND MEDIEVAL BRITAIN

LIFE AND WORK TO THE CLOSE OF THE MIDDLE AGES

T. K. DERRY
M.A. D.PHIL (OXON.)

M. G. BLAKEWAY
M.A. (CANTAB.)

JOHN MURRAY · LONDON

CONTENTS

How Britain Began

Medieval English Society

The Later Middle Ages

PLATES

ACKNOWLEDGEMENTS

Thanks are due to the following who have kindly permitted the reproduction of copyright illustrations:

Plate 1 (photograph by Edwin Smith, copyright Gordon Fraser Gallery Ltd.); 2 (Trinity College, Cambridge); 3 (National Gallery); 4 (Country Life); 5 (Bodleian Library, Oxford); 6, 7, 9, 12, 13, 14, 15, 23 (Trustees of the British Museum); 8 (Wigtown County Library); 10, 16, 20, 21, 25 (Mansell Collection); 11 (International Wool Secretariat); 17 (Clerk of Records, House of Lords); 18 (City Art Gallery, Bristol); 19 (Crown copyright. By permission of the Controller, H.M. Stationery Office. Photograph: National Monuments Record of Scotland); 22 (Trustees of the London Museum); 24 (National Monuments Record); 26 (Worcester College Library, Oxford).

HOW BRITAIN BEGAN

I

THE EARLIEST INHABITANTS

The British people of the present day are the heirs of their predecessors from the beginnings of the permanent settlement of this
island, and still carry some of their blood. More importantly, the
use these earlier occupants made of the land in some measure
affects the use we, their successors, make of the same land. The
tools, too, with which we win our livelihood upon its surface can
be traced back, step by step, to the laborious processes by which
man first equipped himself with the implements of stone and wood
that made his actions more effective than those of the mere animal.

Most of the story belongs to prehistory, that is to say, to the
long centuries for which we have no written records. We must rely
instead upon the picture which archaeologists can form from
surviving evidence of human activity – durable tools and weapons;
the contents of burial places; bones and other food remains and
broken pottery; ornamental objects, carvings, and sometimes
drawings; traces and, occasionally, actual relics of early habita-
tions. Although recent scientific advances make it possible to
date most of this material within a margin of two or three hundred
years, and also to know when important changes of climate and
vegetation took place, only an outline story can be constructed –
and much of that is unverifiable. In particular, because these communities lacked the art of writing they leave us guessing about the
reasons for what they did. Their leaders and forms of government,
ambitions in war and peace, moral standards and religious

1

aspirations can never be made clear from scattered physical relics of the distant past.

How distant it is! The first evidences of human life in our corner of Europe date back thousands of centuries, a length of time with which the imagination cannot grapple. Perhaps this does not matter very seriously, since the remains so far discovered from the oldest and longest period are, as we shall notice, very slight. But when we come to study better-known phases in the later prehistory of Britain, it may help to bear in mind the following comparison. Some general of imperial Rome, travelling across Salisbury Plain after a visit to the famous baths at Aquae Sulis, on the site of modern Bath, may well have paused at Avebury and Stonehenge to puzzle over the ancient stone circles: they were already as old in his day as Aquae Sulis and Hadrian's Wall are in ours.

Men of the Old Stone Age

The earliest men, or near-ancestors of modern man, came northwards into the region of southern Britain about half a million years ago; this was during a long period of increasing warmth. They retreated south again when the returning ice-cap stretched across the midlands; the animals they hunted then sought easier surroundings, and man followed. Even when conditions were most favourable, the population is unlikely to have exceeded a few hundreds, made up of widely scattered family groups roaming about in search of live game and dead carcasses; they also picked berries, nuts, and wild plants, and grubbed up edible roots. There is something pathetic about the multi-purpose stone tools through which we chiefly know them, so painfully long and arduous was the process by which they were gradually improved. Lumps of flint and other hard stones were struck out and shaped with increasing efficiency, but each increase in skill may represent the work of centuries, perhaps whole millennia, of trial and error. The few camp sites still recognizable (such as that at Cuxton in Kent) were located by lakes or rivers, but apart from the evidence of tool-making they suggest lairs rather than homes.

When the ice spread southwards for the third and last time

during the prehistory of man, somewhere about sixty thousand years ago, the enormously long 'lower palaeolithic' age with its almost imperceptible rate of progress came at last to an end. In the 'upper palaeolithic' age which followed, the type of man from whom modern men are descended is clearly present, displaying a new-found ability to adapt himself to extremes of cold. These are the people whose winter-season homes can be traced in the caves of Cheddar Gorge, the Gower Peninsula, and Creswell Crags in Derbyshire. For tools they had sharp-edged 'blades' and other shapes of stone which they adapted to special purposes; they also made extensive use of bone and antler. They were able to make clothes of animal fur and roughly dressed skins, and enjoyed further protection against the weather through knowing how to kindle and control a fire. In addition, their success as reindeer hunters means that they must have acquired some at least of the special techniques employed for this purpose by the modern Lapps.

Yet it was surely a bleak existence for them near the edge of the ice. During a period which lasted for about fifty thousand years it is likely that the population of Britain never exceeded a couple of thousand and was often reduced to much less. Although remains show that the dead were carefully buried and that the living possessed ornaments, such as animal-tooth necklaces, development seems to have fallen behind that of lands a little farther south. In particular, Britain has only a few small bone engravings to show from the period when the caves of the Pyrenees were being decked with astonishingly realistic portrayals of hunting scenes, drawn no doubt with magical intent.

In the course of the tenth and ninth millennia B.C. the ice sheets finally retreated, and men adapted themselves again to a fresh environment. In new forests of pine and birch they hunted the red deer, and it seems probable that the dog was now domesticated and helped in the chase. They used spears and arrows tipped with carefully shaped flint points, such as figure in museums as 'microliths'. Their most important new tools were the stone axe and inward-curving adze, with which forest-dwellers felled trees, fashioned rough dwellings, hollowed out boats from tree trunks, and equipped themselves with various gear for hunting, fowling, and fishing. Other, less well provided groups, including those who were perhaps the earliest inhabitants of Scotland, lived, partly on shellfish, along the shore-line. A population of about ten thousand has been suggested for this intermediate or 'mesolithic' form of society.

Though numbers were no doubt on the increase, it was still a very thinly peopled Britain which, somewhere between 6000 and 5000 B.C., acquired for the first time the character of an island and its present shape. The melting of glaciers, and the rise in the earth's crust which accompanied it, caused a great surge of water in northern Europe. The North Sea flooded in over a vast area of river bed and swamp; the North Channel was formed between Scotland and Ireland; and the English Channel, though it long continued to be narrower than it is now, made the separation from the mainland complete. The changes in sea level may have been partly responsible for an increase in the rain and mist reaching the new island from the Atlantic, which gave the islanders forests of oak and alder in place of pine and birch and impeded the river valleys with endless morasses. Since two later climatic changes, which will be noticed in due course, had less far-reaching effects, we may say that the inhabitants of Britain were now face to face with the physical conditions which largely shaped their life during the remaining millennia of prehistory – and which still influence our activities today.

Apart from the effect of climate and the insular position, the most significant of those conditions was the broad contrast between the lowlands of the south and east and the highlands of the north and west. Comparatively speaking, the one is dry, warm, and fertile country, the other wet, cold, and infertile. Moreover, the lowlands are more easily accessible from the continent by short sea crossings which lead to an inviting coastline. Their chalk and limestone hills and ridges were feasible for travel by primitive men and attractive for settlement. Later on, means were found for taming and draining their forests and water-logged valleys, whereas the heath and scrub of the highland zone never repaid cultivation. In any age, the lowlands presented a familiar and hopeful appearance to pioneers from western Europe in search of new homes. Not so the mountains and moors.

While we shall have occasion to notice some entries made directly into the north and west by sea, the highland population was to consist mainly of groups that had moved away from the lowlands, either driven out by superior forces or quietly withdrawing to avoid contact with new and unwelcome ways of living. In the remoter parts of Wales and Scotland the observant visitor may still see traces of a conservative attitude which may have very ancient origins. But since Britain was on the edge of the continent and the mountainous zones were on the edge of Britain, neither people nor ideas could permanently escape intermixture; so the long-term result has often been a compromise between old and new.

During the last three millennia of Britain's prehistory, to which we shall now turn, immigrant groups of varying size and significance brought many innovations to the island. Our attention can only be given to a few of them, namely those which seem to have made the biggest impact. But it is important to bear in mind throughout that each successive change could only gradually displace established ways of living. Even in the south, old and new must have existed side by side for several generations at least, and in the least accessible districts of the north the time lag might be as much as a thousand years.

The Neolithic Revolution

About 3200 B.C. the arrival of the first few farmers upon our shores began a change of such tremendous importance that it has been called the 'neolithic revolution'. This was the introduction of life in settled communities, which first became possible when, instead of roaming in search of his food, man began to reap crops of his own sowing and to domesticate some of the animals he had been accustomed to pursue. Both these ideas travelled very slowly onwards to our island from regions in eastern Europe, to which they had spread nearly two thousand years earlier from their places of origin in the Middle East. By the time that agriculture was beginning in a very small way in Britain, in Egypt and Mesopotamia it had already provided the basis for urban civilizations with a recorded history.

The methods of tillage employed by our earliest settlers have left few traces, for they had no ploughs with which to cultivate regular fields. Instead, they made clearings on thin woodland, such as then covered even the downs, but cutting and burning the undergrowth, branches, and as much as they could manage of the trunks of the trees. The wood ash helped to fertilize the soil, which they scratched up with wooden hoes and rakes sufficiently for it to bear a few crops of wheat or possibly barley; these they harvested with stone sickles. As soon as one patch ceased to bear, another would be cleared. A small kind of apple tree was also planted out from a very early date at the edge of the woods, possibly for cider.

But the keeping of cattle and pigs, which could flourish on forest ground, and perhaps a few goats and sheep, almost certainly played a larger part. This is indicated by the size of the 'causewayed camps' of this period, whose palisaded banks must have been used as enclosures for stock: at Windmill Hill in Wiltshire, a triple ring encircles twenty acres. All this would be combined with man's older activities of hunting and foraging, which now included a great deal of foliage-cutting and bark-stripping to provide cattle-food for the winter.

Living in settled communities, the people had more chance of developing skill in handicrafts. The women added ornament to the first rough, bag-shaped pottery, which was kneaded by hand and fired on the domestic hearth; they were also expert in basketry and leather-work. But it must have been very much an 'age of wood', since there were trees in abundance almost everywhere and the finely polished stone axe which was now in use was adequate both for felling and for shaping the timber to make huts and most of their contents. Its quality depended partly upon having suitable flint or other hard stone, so roughed-out axeheads were obtained by barter trade from districts where the material was available. The thirty-foot-deep mines at Grimes Graves in Norfolk, where flints were prised out with antler picks, and the stone-littered mountain-side at Craig Llwyd in North Wales were among the chief sites of Britain's oldest industry; the Welsh product reached as far afield as Essex. Though hardly any traces of their hut homes survive, these early farmers built themselves a memorial in the 'long barrows', mounds of earth as much as several hundred feet in length, raised originally over many bodies. These are still to be seen along the downs and as far north as Yorkshire.

Another group of early agricultural settlers is known to us only through the survival of their 'megalithic graves'. These are stone-built galleries or chambers, originally perhaps covered with earth but now conspicuous for the huge size of some of the blocks of which they are composed. They could house many corpses and, unlike the long barrows, could easily be re-opened: some were in use over a period of a thousand years (c. 3000–2000 B.C.). Since very few megalithic graves are to be found in the generally favoured south and east of the island, it seems clear that their builders did not mingle readily with the farming population already in possession. But they occur in great numbers all along the western and northern coasts, with a maximum concentration of fifty in the Scilly Isles, which suggests that they were the work of a maritime people.

They brought their practices with them from the western Mediterranean and spread them widely in France. From Britain and Ireland they went on to Denmark and the shores of the Baltic. But whether they came as conquerors or traders or missionaries of a vanished faith is a mystery that has given rise to many theories, none of which has been satisfactorily proved.

Near the close of the third millennium B.C., after an improvement of climate had encouraged the spread of farming among the older populations of the island, two new peoples began to arrive. The smaller group, which may have come from western France, is identified by its practice of cremating the dead before individual burial; but it is best known to us through one of its settlements, at Skara Brae in the Orkneys. The lack of trees in the wind-swept islands caused the eight huts and their furnishings to be made of stone, and in this lonely situation they still remain to give the first glimpse of a prehistoric domestic interior. The living-room, about sixteen feet square, has a central hearth (for peat), box beds, a seat, and a kind of dresser. Each dwelling is adjoined by a small store-room and linked with its neighbours by covered passages; there are slabstone drains.

The larger group are known as the Bell-Beaker people, from the

drinking vessel which they placed in graves and intended presumably as a kind of stirrup-cup for the journey to the world
beyond. Their way of life or culture originated in the Iberian
Peninsula, but the people who brought it entered Britain from
various parts of the continent, possibly bringing with them also
the first Indo-European language to be spoken here. They raised
the earliest 'round barrows' and round cairns over their distinguished dead, and erected the first stone circles and other align-
ments of stones. They share responsibility with the smaller group
(referred to above) for a further development, called the 'henge',
which is not found in ritual structures outside the island. This was
a system of oval or circular ditches and banks, used to delimit the
sacred area within which stone circles or other revered objects lay.
At Avebury the ditch and bank each had an original perpendicular
measurement of thirty feet, so as to enclose the vast stone circle
within an area of nearly thirty acres. At Stonehenge the 'henge'
was on a much more modest scale, but the site must have achieved
high sanctity when the Beaker people placed within it an incom-
plete circle of 'bluestones'. Not only had these been fetched from
the Prescelly Hills in far-off Pembrokeshire, but it is believed that
their place of origin was already sacred.

Plate 1. *Interior of a hut at Skara Brae, Orkney Isles.* The hearth is in the centre
and the beds (probably originally filled with heather or bracken) to left and right.
A two-shelved dresser is at the back. At Rinyo, on Roushay island nearby, similar
huts have been uncovered which, like those at Skara Brae, were preserved by
being covered over with storm-blown sand. (Cf. text p. 7.)

Plate 2. *The White Horse and Uffington Castle, Berkshire.* The iron-age White Horse
and 'Castle' are here backed by the Berkshire Ridgeway (running from the top left
corner to the middle of the right-hand edge of the picture) – a track which is part
of the general system of the Icknield Way (at least Iron-Age and probably older),
connecting Berkshire with Norfolk. The Castle is one of several hill-forts in the
south and south east of England which were unfinished, probably because of a
scare from a later wave of invaders. (Cf. text pp. 15 and 12.)

Plate 3. *Bonze Shield from the Thames at Battersea.* First century B.C., or early
first century A.D. (now in the British Museum). Its curvilinear and abstract decoration is typically La Tène and includes studs set with red glass and pinned in position.
(Cf. text p. 15.)

Plate 4. *The Desborough Mirror.* First century A.D. from Desborough, Northamptonshire, and now in the British Museum, where it can be compared with a
similar mirror from Birdlip, Gloucestershire – both fine examples of La Tène
abstract pattens. (Cf. text p. 15.)

Plates 1 and 2

Plate 3

Plate 4

So little is known about the settlements of the Beaker people, as opposed to their places of presumed worship, that they are thought to have been to some extent nomads, moving about the downland with their herds and flocks. For crops, they grew barley rather than wheat and to some extent cultivated flax, though the fact that they have left behind buttons but not pins shows that they dressed in leather and furs rather than textiles. Most important of all as regards the future, the Beaker people brought the first metal objects to the island and prospected for ores of copper and gold, which were now in high demand on the continent.

The Bronze Age

Soon after 2000 B.C., Britain began slowly to move into the Bronze Age. It was becoming more and more widely known that copper alloyed with about one-tenth tin was both stronger and easier to cast than copper alone, with the result that Central European bronze-users in search of new supplies of metal carried their technical knowledge with them into the British Isles. The first native bronze industries then grew up near sources of metal in Ireland and in the highland zone of Britain. One important trade route now ran from Ireland to Scandinavia via northern Scotland, which had its own copper and may have imported tin for the Scottish bronzes from Bohemia through the Rhine valley. Still more important, however, was the trade route across south-west England, which supplied the continent with Irish gold, Irish and Welsh copper, and the now enormously valuable Cornish tin.

Before the middle of the second millennium B.C. the opportunity had been seized by a warrior people to establish a rich and powerful aristocratic rule in Wessex, which gradually extended over most of southern and eastern England. They may have come from Brittany, and it is possible that the first bronze-smiths to work in southern Britain accompanied them. Certainly these warriors plied daggers, rapiers, and axes of bronze. Their leaders lie buried under elaborate round barrows, with highly decorated staffs of office and gold-ornamented ceremonial weapons. The jewels which their long-dead ladies wore included jet from the Yorkshire coast, amber brought by the great trade route from the

Baltic to Central Europe, and beads of glass and blue faience which originated in the civilization of the Aegean. Such were the profits derived from the exploitation of an embryonic European Common Market.

But the great glory of the Wessex chieftains is the vastness and sublimity of the work they did at Stonehenge. The rearranged 'bluestones' are dwarfed by the sandstone 'sarsens', weighing up to sixty tons, which form the great circle and the horseshoe-shaped setting of the five trilithons erected within. Even in their ruined condition they are still an awe-inspiring sight. By what means the horizontal stones were lifted into position is disputed, but there can be no doubt that those who planned and carried out the scheme controlled a large and disciplined labour force, which must have been available – perhaps at certain seasons only – over a very long period of time. As for the purposes served by this unique structure, it is generally supposed that people from a wide area travelled to Stonehenge along the well-established trackways over the downs for religious celebrations, which may well have included a form of sun worship. The opening in the central horse-shoe of stones is aligned with a monolith outside, marking the exact direction of sunrise on midsummer day; whether this was the scene and occasion of human sacrifices can neither be proved nor disproved. Recent theories, based on computer analysis, have tried to show that Stonehenge as a whole is laid out on a precise astronomical basis, and have at least established that its constructors were more aware of the orderliness of sun and moon phases than was previously thought possible.

In the following period (from c. 1400 B.C.) the use of bronze was further developed, and the bronze-smiths must have formed a special class of highly respected craftsmen. Sheet metal was produced for the first time, and ornamental castings were made by the elaborate *cire perdue* method. This required the use of a mould shaped round a wax interior, which was subsequently melted and replaced by the molten metal. When work of this kind was possible, it is easy to understand that the fighting man was at last supplied with a sword strong enough for slashing, and that a whole new range of more efficient tools became available for carpentry and other peacetime skills. Wooden ploughs were brought into use for the cross-ploughing which created the first squarish fields, misleadingly called 'Celtic'. The livestock now included some horses and an increasing number of sheep; the latter fact suggests that weaving became an important activity. Crops were still grown chiefly on the downland, but it is the eastern slopes of Dartmoor which happen to provide the best surviving specimens of circular hut sites from this period, clustered sometimes within a perimeter wall. The conclusion seems to be that the agricultural unit was a single self-sufficient farmstead rather than a hamlet or village.

Some new groups in the population have been identified by the various types of urn, containing the ashes of the dead and often assembled in cemeteries. These new waves of immigrants may have been the forerunners of the big Celtic immigrations of later times. In any case, their arrival did not apparently hamper the gradual diffusion among poorer classes and in remoter areas of something like a common level of culture. At 'Jarlshof', a stone-built settlement in the Shetlands, the remains even enable the archaeologist to trace the coming of the first bronze-smith and the impact of the first bronze-smithy at one of the farthest points of Bronze Age Britain.

The Coming of the Celts

In the sixth century the last phase of British prehistory began with the first large-scale incursion of the Celts. These were the people whom Pytheas of Marseilles, our earliest known visitor from the civilized world, must have met in about 325 B.C. and whom Julius Caesar later found in possession of the island. They form an important element in the make-up of its modern population, particularly in the west and north. The oldest surviving names of physical features are of Celtic origin. They occur most frequently in rivers: Thames, Trent, and Severn are all Celtic names, and Axe, Esk, Exe, and Usk variants of the Celtic word for 'water'. Indeed, the Celts as a whole are less satisfactorily defined by any racial characteristics than by their language, from which are descended Welsh (with Breton as its offshoot) and the Gaelic of Ireland and northern Scotland. They were regarded by the Romans as a very warlike people, having emerged from their earlier homes in south Germany to intimidate much of the continent; their power was felt as far afield as Asia Minor in the one direction and Italy and the Iberian Peninsula in the other.

The Celts were among the earliest users of iron in central Europe, and the well-hammered iron sword which outclassed all earlier weapons was in their hands when they first invaded Britain. This seems to have been an invasion by a peasant class, who spread themselves widely through the English lowlands. Their culture, as shown for example in types of pottery, belongs to an early stage in Iron Age development, known from one of its Austrian centres as 'Hallstatt'. About two centuries later, however, a second Celtic invasion brought in a much more advanced culture, known to us for a similar reason as 'La Tène' and represented by most of the admired pieces of Celtic workmanship in modern museums.

The second body of invaders, who came from the region of the Marne into the south and especially the east, and also from Brittany into the south-west, included war bands. They brought the horse-drawn chariot into use on the field of battle, and it was in the struggle against them that the hill fort became a prominent feature of many landscapes. On a steeply sloping site successive rings of ditches, earthen banks and palisades could make the position almost impregnable, and the great size of many of the enclosures shows that they were designed as places of refuge for the entire neighbouring population with all their cattle.

Since iron ore, at least in the form of bog-iron, was available in most parts of the country, simply equipped smithies must soon have become widespread. Ploughs with iron-tipped shares made it possible to extend the cultivated area by taking in land deforested with the sharp iron axe. Large quantities of a hardier type of wheat were now grown, though a worsening of the climate in the last half-millennium B.C. often made it necessary to dry the grain under cover after cutting it unripe. New crops at this period included beans, and the more general use of vegetable food was a reason for the establishment of the first salt-workings along the coast. The farm cart must presumably have been introduced along with the chariot, both of which increased the demand for horses, while reduction of the forest area also meant more room for sheep.

The huts of the Celtic inhabitants of Britain continued to have a generally round shape. They often included storage pits and a courtyard, and while many farmsteads were isolated, there is evidence of the growth of hamlets and even villages. At Glastonbury and Meare in the Somersetshire marshes, excavation has revealed the existence of two villages built up on wooden piers above the water. They would be safe from casual marauders and at the same time accessible to waterborne trade: we know that dug-out canoes had now been supplemented in some parts by plank boats, skilfully sewn together with withies, and there were doubtless other types as well. The Glastonbury settlement had sixty hearths, and the people who once sat or crouched beside them were leather-workers, wood turners, wheelwrights, cloth weavers, makers of wicker baskets, and practisers of many other part-time handicrafts.

Somewhere about the year 100 B.C., the region of the lower Thames valley began to be entered by a tribe known to Caesar as the Belgae; they had moved into Gaul from Germany more recently than the Celts, with whom they were partly intermingled. In spite of the hill forts, many of which were given additional embankments at this time for protection against Belgic slings, these people forced their way into Kent, East Anglia, the midlands, and even the south-west. Their coming was doubly important. On the one hand, they introduced more advanced ways of living. The Belgae brought to the island a heavy plough with an iron coulter, which enabled the stiff clays to be cultivated. They had wheel-thrown, kiln-dried pottery; replaced an iron-bar currency, which could not circulate fast or far, by proper coinage; and they even learnt to copy the rotary querns with which the Roman soldiers ground their corn ration. The capitals of their little kingdoms bore some resemblance to towns, inasmuch as a large number of huts were assembled in a single fortified area. On the other hand, the close relations which the Belgae in Britain maintained with their fellow-tribesmen in Gaul provided the pretext for Caesar's invasion.

The Island as Known by Julius Caesar

In the August of 55 B.C., Caesar made a foray with a force of about 10,000 men against the Belgae of eastern Kent, returning the next year with a larger expedition, which stormed an embanked capital in Hertfordshire. In his *De Bello Gallico* Caesar gives a more detailed account than we possess for any other single episode in our early history. He also made the name of the island 'Britannia', which previous writers had first called 'Albion' and then one of the 'Pretanic Isles'. For another century it was allowed to relapse into unrecorded obscurity, linked with the all-powerful Roman world by no ties except those of trade. But the exports of raw materials, which included chain-gangs of hapless slaves, and the imports of luxuries, including large amphoras of Italian wine for feasting chieftains, made conquest some day inevitable.

Before ancient Britain passes into Roman Britain, there are two aspects of Celtic (including Belgic) life which deserve some mention. One is their strongly held religion, presided over by a class of priestly soothsayers, the 'druids'. Very little is known about its beliefs, but the worshippers assembled in sacred oak groves, which were the scene of grisly human sacrifices; a few wooden idols survive; and there is evidence of valuable votive offerings made to their deities by the waterside. The celebration of May Day and the cult of the mistletoe are also traditionally associated with the religion of the Celts. Their artistic achievements, too, must often have had a religious basis which we can only very dimly discern.

Their performances in the arts are the aspect of Celtic life which shows these people at their most talented. They had no advanced technical civilization, but a feeling for beauty which civilized man may envy. Much of their artistic skill went to the embellishment either of elaborate war equipment or of personal ornaments, in either case the possessions mainly of a wealthy aristocracy, such as that which came to eastern England from the region of the Marne. But the bronze bowls and buckets, the brooches, and the decorated pottery of the Somersetshire lake villages show that beauty of design was not restricted to an aristocratic minority.

The artistic objects surviving were wrought chiefly in bronze, gold, or enamel inlays, but sometimes in other materials, including iron and even shale. Their most characteristic feature is the use of remarkable abstract designs, based on the spiral and open circle. Human and animal figures appear rather rarely, and are stylized rather than realistic. The mirrors with their delightfully engraved backs strike more homely chords, since we should only require to replace the polished metal front by glass to produce an article which could stand unchallenged on a modern dressing-table. But perhaps the Uffington White Horse, which has given its name to the Berkshire vale, links us still more closely, since the piety of fifty or sixty successive generations has kept the turf from encroaching on this emblem of some long-forgotten cult. The animal is only the suggestion of a horse and is like none known to nature – and all the more powerful and lively for that.

Some of the loveliest ornaments, including hoarded gold, survive because they were buried for safety during the troubled first century B.C. Other items, such as a famous bronze shield-cover taken from the Thames at Battersea, show that, even before the Romans conquered the island, trade relations were causing their artistically inferior products to be imitated, so that the lines of Celtic art flowed less gracefully. Both events foreshadowed the great change which was about to come over the relatively free and disordered life of Celtic Britain.

2

ROMAN BRITAIN

In A.D. 43 the time arrived when the Romans, under the emperor
Claudius, decided that Britain would make a convenient and
profitable addition to the empire. The task was entrusted to four
legions, containing some 25,000 first-class soldiers and about
15,000 lighter-armed auxiliaries. The lowlands were quickly
overrun. Although some of the strongly entrenched hill forts of
the south-west, such as Maiden Castle, had to be taken by storm,
within half a dozen years the earliest of several campaigns into
Wales was already in progress from a front whose lateral communications ran approximately along the line still marked by the
Roman Fosse Way; temporary headquarters for the legions were
established at Gloucester and Lincoln. Peaceful development was,
indeed, interrupted by the famous revolt under Boudicca in 61,
when Roman settlements at Colchester, London, and St Albans
all went up in flames, but heavy punishments prevented any
repetition.

As for the hill districts, Wales was conquered piecemeal, and
the numerous and turbulent Brigantes, who held most of northern
England, were reduced to some semblance of order by advances
along both flanks of the Pennines. Scotland presented the biggest
problem, which was firmly tackled during the governorship of
Agricola, of which we have a detailed account in a memoir by his
son-in-law, the great Roman historian Tacitus. He based one of his
legions as far north as Inchtuthil, on the left bank of the Spey,
and after a further advance in the direction of the Moray Firth,
he won a pitched battle over a tribal confederacy in A.D. 84 at the
unidentified 'Mons Graupius'. But events in other parts of the
empire caused one legion to be permanently withdrawn and
another had to be replaced after a savage outbreak among the
Brigantes, with the result that the regular limit of occupation was

fixed by the emperor Hadrian at the wall which he ordered to be built from the Solway to the Tyne. For part of the second century the frontier moved forward again, to a much shorter wall constructed between the Clyde and the Forth, and there were also brief periods when it bent in the opposite direction as tribesmen surged past Hadrian's Wall to join forces with the Brigantes beyond. But in general the great wall and its outlying forts in the hinterland to the north isolated the unconquered tribes sufficiently for the Romans to keep order in the hill districts lying farther south, and so to maintain the necessary conditions for civilized life to flourish in the lowlands of southern and eastern Britain.

Military Control

Thus the province at all times included a military zone, in which the principal feature was Hadrian's Wall, the most striking artificial boundary in the whole empire. All three legions and a mass of conscript labour shared in its construction, which took about eight years (125–133) to complete. The wall itself, eventually stone-built throughout, had a minimum thickness of eight feet and a height of twelve, with a deep external ditch except where a natural precipice was available. Milecastles and frequent turrets housed the troops on patrol duty and protected the gateways, while sixteen permanent forts provided accommodation for a maximum garrison of about 35,000 men. On the south side access to the region of the wall was obstructed by a wide, flat-bottomed ditch, to make sure that there was no illicit trade or communication from within the province. The gates could be used for authorized commerce in either direction, but they also acted as sallyports, so that raiding barbarians could be rounded up against the wall for easy annihilation by missiles from the top. It is significant that the supreme command was exercised from the west end of the wall area, where there were also forts to cover the sea approaches from unconquered Ireland.

The legions had their bases at York, Chester, and Caerleon, where they were within easy marching distance of the mountains and had good communications by water as well as by road. The walled enclosures of the fortresses were soon adjoined by the dwellings of a civilian population which traded with the well-paid legionaries. But regiments of auxiliaries, who had lighter arms, less training, and smaller pay than the legions, and were therefore more readily expendable, were thinly spread over a much wider area. They occupied a network of at least a hundred small forts, reaching far into the recesses of Wales and the Pennines, from which they overawed potential troublemakers, took the first shock of any rising, and safeguarded communications along the roads.

At least two thousand miles of roads were built, especially during the early part of the occupation when military and administrative needs were most urgent. They traversed the whole of the civil and most of the military zone, from the Channel ports to the Wall, and radiated like the spokes of a wheel from the lowest crossing of the Thames at London. Thus they ran along the Thames valley to Silchester and the west; north-west to North Wales and Chester by the Watling Street, intersecting the Fosse Way near the centre of England; north by the Ermine Street[1] to Lincoln and York; and north-east to Colchester and the neighbourhood of Norwich. Civil and military officials, orders and dispatches, supplies and reinforcements were sped quickly across the province, which eventually had sixteen imperial post routes, with vehicles and posting-stations maintained by the local authorities for government use. In the military zone, too, lesser roads joined fort with fort, and gave the legions rapid access both to the Wall and to any other area where punitive operations might be required.

When necessary, the legionaries did their own road-building, but generally manual labour was conscripted locally to work under military engineers and supervisors, who set out the course by alignment from a series of high points. Straightness was therefore combined with steep gradients, but the surface was superb both for wheeled traffic and marching men. The bed was placed on top of a raised earthwork, thus providing drainage on both sides; its width varied with the importance of the thoroughfare, from twenty-four down to fifteen feet or less; whatever material was available was lavishly used to make a whole series of layers; and they were carefully compacted so that the final result was as hard

[1] The three names are Anglo-Saxon, not Romano-British.

and impervious as nineteenth-century macadam. The upkeep of the roads was part of the price Rome exacted from her subjects as their contribution to the cost of the Roman Peace.

The south and east of the island enjoyed something like three centuries of virtually uninterrupted peace, during which many districts lying off the main roads may never even have seen a company of soldiers. It is true that some Britons were recruited to serve the empire abroad at quite an early period, and that the garrison of the island eventually included a large home-born element. But taking the occupation as a whole, this uniquely durable peace was maintained by Romans for Britons as a necessary condition for the profitable exploitation of conquered territory.

Exploitation

It is significant that the supreme military and civil authority of the governor did not cover revenue, for which a special official called the procurator was directly answerable to the emperor. There were taxes in money and kind, and the customs duties levied on trade across the frontier constituted an important reason for the closely guarded gates on the Wall. Large supplies of corn were needed for the garrison in the military zone, to which it was conveyed by road or river or, from the fens, by the canals which the Romans built to drain the land. Much of this corn was obtained by a tax on native farms, which is calculated to have amounted at times to as much as three-fifths of the crop. In addition, there were imperial agricultural estates, worked presumably by a bailiff in charge of a large force of dependent workers.

But the Romans were more keenly interested in exploiting the mineral wealth, which had long been a known feature of the island. Lead, copper, tin, iron, coal, and – at one Welsh site – gold were all mined during the Roman period, though partly of course for domestic uses. Cornish tin had little value for the empire at large until the middle of the third century, when the Spanish supply ran out, and it had plenty of other iron-producing centres. Welsh copper, however, helped to maintain the output of Roman bronzes, while the demand for lead was practically unlimited. Lead smelting was the only source for their supply of silver; alloyed with tin, it provided pewter for many domestic vessels; and Roman plumbing, which was extensive, relied on lead for the most important pipes and other fittings. Lead was therefore mined in the Mendips, Derbyshire, Flintshire, Yorkshire, and elsewhere, partly by private firms but under imperial control and licence.

More generally, both the export and the import trade of the province benefited an influential capitalist class: the philosopher Seneca, who also carried weight as a millionaire-senator, was alleged to have placed loans so widely in Britain that his decision to call in his money was one cause of Boudicca's revolt. It was inevitable that the exports of a new and distant province should be chiefly raw materials, but the garments of woollen cloth, which found a sale in the eastern half of the empire, may not have been the only manufactures in which the people of the damp island were later found to excel. Superior-quality pottery, for instance, was at first imported; then made for the home market at such centres as Castor, where the Ermine Street crosses the Nene; and eventually Castor ware was selling as far away as the Rhineland. Wine and olive oil, however, were products which did not admit of successful local imitation. Together with luxury goods of many kinds, from glassware to fine furniture, their importation provided steady profits to the merchants who always followed in the footsteps of the Roman armies.

Once the province had been pacified, the growth of its internal industry and commerce created new wealth, of which a part went to the imperial authorities in taxation. In return, Britain profited by the spread into the north of new techniques, including even the use of water-power for grinding corn, which was introduced by the soldiers at the Wall and is clearly traceable elsewhere. But the new technique which did most to stimulate economic life was undoubtedly the creation of towns.

Town Life

The Romans believed in towns as a civilizing and unifying influence for holding together the whole of their tremendous empire. Their word for 'city' gives us two adjectives, 'urban' and 'urbane', which taken together remind us that to them city life did not only mean the security and purely material advantages of a large community and its organization through some special form of local self-government: it also implied the spread of refined manners and a polished society. Town building in Britain was therefore a deliberate policy: townspeople might learn to wear the Roman *toga* (as Tacitus suggests), and even the poorer classes made some use of the Latin language. During the initial period of construction, estimated at twenty or twenty-five years, public money was probably made available for the most important buildings and the characteristic rectangular street-pattern laid out by military engineers and masons. Such is the likely origin of local centres, where the Celtic aristocracy could be romanized and traders and craftsmen would automatically follow their lead. But the most important towns were, of course, those which the central authorities, civil and military, required for their own purposes.

At the very outset the Romans developed a capital at Colchester, built on a site adjacent to that of the sprawling Celtic hut town which the emperor Claudius himself had entered in triumph in A.D. 43. Its most striking feature was a great temple for the Roman cult of emperor worship, but this was not rebuilt with the rest of the city after the devastation inflicted by Boudicca. By the end of the first century, however, the procurator at least was based in London, which marked itself out as the most suitable location for a capital. London grew up as a natural centre for trade, favoured perhaps by Roman merchants even before the conquest. The river gave an excellent approach for shipping from the continent. Two low hills on the left bank, not far from the limits to which the tide reaches, indicated a likely site for a settlement, which had the further advantage that patches of gravel on both banks made the crossing of the river easy. A ford, and later presumably a bridge, from which (as we have seen) the roads were made to radiate conveniently in all directions, complete the list of commercial assets that made London a great city. In the fourth century it received the honorific title of *Augusta*, and although the population may not have exceeded an estimated 15,000, its area of 326 acres

made it one of the largest towns in all the northern provinces of
the empire. A few stretches of the massive walls still stand, but
most of Roman London lies securely buried under the City of
London which occupies much the same site.

The administration of northern Britain, which at one time
became a separate province, was centred upon York, where – as at
Chester and Caerleon – a town grew up inevitably around the
headquarters of a legion. Together with Colchester, Lincoln, and
Gloucester, it also achieved the rank of a *colonia*, that is, a place of
settlement for retired legionaries, who were given a house in the
town and land outside which they could cultivate. Since legionaries were men of substance, who had always had the status of
Roman citizens, the four *coloniae* and St Albans, which may have
had the rank of a chartered city or *municipium*, became natural
centres of romanization. At St Albans the public buildings included
a theatre, at Lincoln the amenities extended to an underground
system of sewers, and all five were eventually provided with
elaborate walls and fine gateways.

Cantonal Capitals

But a more widespread influence was exercised upon the Celtic
population through the cantonal capitals, set up to administer the
affairs of the different tribes. Each had a network of local roads,
making it a natural centre for trade. The chessboard pattern of
streets offered ample space for the town houses of a gentry class,
whom business of many kinds brought to the centre of local affairs
and who were tempted to reside there for part of each year because
of its social attractions. In addition, a walled town, such as these
became in troubled times, offered full protection against roaming
marauders. About a dozen of these county towns, as we might
fairly call them, can be identified. In the south, Canterbury,
Chichester, Winchester, Silchester, Cirencester, Dorchester, and
Exeter; beyond these, Caerwent, Caister-by-Norwich, Leicester,
and Wroxeter; in the north, only Aldborough. Since the size and
ground-plan remain fairly constant, it will be sufficient to describe
Silchester, where the absence of modern buildings has made
thorough excavation possible.

The original 200-acre site is irregular in shape, and may have been partly inhabited before the Roman period; in the second century it was reduced by half, yet remained quite adequate for the population, which never exceeded a very few thousands. It was latterly enclosed by a wall, which had six gates and a postern. Nearly two acres were occupied by the colonnaded forum, having a monumental gateway at one end and at the other an imposing basilica, where the lawcourts and cantonal council meetings were held. There were four temples, which were probably dedicated to Celtic divinities who passed under partly Roman names. The neighbourhood of the forum also contains one of the very few known sites of an early Christian church. Other public buildings included a large bath-house, with rooms maintained at various temperatures by underfloor heating; an amphitheatre, located outside the walls; and an official guest-house or *mansio*, used in connection with the imperial posting-system. The streets, which intersect strictly at right-angles, were bordered by about fifty houses big enough to have served as the residences of the local aristocracy or prosperous merchants, and by numerous small shops and workplaces. There are also many apparently vacant spaces, which may well have been occupied by the timber dwellings of the humbler classes.

Bath – and to a much smaller extent Buxton – had a special position due to the hot springs, which attracted visitors in search of a cure for rheumatism and other ailments, or merely for the pleasure of bathing in sociable and luxurious surroundings. The importance of Bath is illustrated by the fact that, in addition to its three great baths, with their ornamental pillars and statuary, it possessed one of the very few temples in the full classical style, dedicated to the local deity, Sul Minerva, whose sacred fire was fed with Mendip coal.

At the other end of the scale, Britain also contained many very small urban centres which sprang up haphazard, where a cross-roads or a nearby military post – as, for instance, in the neighbourhood of the Wall – offered the native population a chance of earning money. But even when allowance is made for all these, it seems clear that the drift to the towns was very much a minority movement. Many of the more prosperous elements in Celtic society may have been enthusiastic imitators of Rome, but it would not be easy to transplant a way of life that had grown up slowly in lands much farther south. It is estimated that townspeople never formed more than about ten per cent of the population of Roman Britain.

Villas and Agriculture

The life of the province centred upon the countryside, where Roman influence spread much more slowly and imperfectly. So long as they kept quiet, the Celts there did not need to learn anything new. In some areas it is clear that they kept the type of homes, fields, and farming practices which they had had before the conquest. In the fens, for instance, the Romans initiated big drainage schemes, but allowed the new agricultural district to be tilled in the old way, as long as the corn requisitions for the army were promptly forthcoming. In the north, too, the herdsmen of the moors often continued their pastoral existence much as before, except that they had to satisfy very big demands for skins to make military equipment and lard for the soldier's ration of fat. Even in those parts of southern England where the Roman influence was strongest, we cannot exclude the possibility that the new romanized farm estates often had numerous backward Celtic smallholdings somewhere in their vicinity.

A romanized farm estate, large or small, centred upon a *villa*. This was the Latin name for the country homes built on the Roman plan, of which nearly seven hundred can still be traced, nine-tenths of them south of the line of the Fosse Way. They occur most frequently on southern slopes in well-drained localities with good access to building-stone. In a few cases, as at Lullingstone in Kent, the size of the rooms and the luxury of their equipment suggest a parallel with the country seats of the nobility and gentry of quite recent centuries. There are also a few where the lay-out and finds indicate that some manufacturing process was carried out on the premises, such as large-scale weaving and fulling of cloth. But in the vast majority of cases the villa is a farmhouse, with its rooms strung out along a corridor or more ambitiously round three sides of a courtyard. Viewed today, the foundations and fragmentary walls make them seem bigger than they actually were, because they were usually single-storied and many of the buildings on a site were only barns and storehouses.

It is likely that some villas housed the bailiff of an imperial estate, and some certainly belonged to retired officials, veterans of the armies, or foreign merchants who invested their money in a residence here. But the most common occupant was a Celt, whose rank or wealth encouraged him to live in Roman style. The agriculture, too, would be Roman, with a mould-board, perhaps, added to the heavy Belgic plough; iron spades and two-handled scythes to make labour more efficient; and improved methods of drying corn. The main crop was wheat, grown in long, open fields which were left fallow in alternate years. Profits were generally good, and it is sometimes possible to trace the way in which some part of them was used to add to the size and comfort of the residence. But practically nothing is known about the workers on the farm, who in the case of the largest estates may have numbered as much as a hundred and who often occupied living accommodation in, or closely adjoining, the villa. Were they slaves or free men? If mainly free, was their labour paid for by wages in cash and food or by crofter holdings? It has been argued that they would not have been allowed to live so close to their master's residence unless their own conditions were tolerable; on the other hand, evidence that infanticide by exposure was a common practice suggests that any increase in their numbers was harshly discouraged.

The villa represented, at least so far as the owner was concerned, a serene and civilized way of living. The principal rooms were set to face the sun, and often had well-proportioned verandas in front. Plastered walls, sometimes decorated with frescoes, looked down on the mosaics which were a more durable substitute for carpeting. The coloured stone cubes, smaller than lumps of sugar, of which they were composed, showed geometrical patterns, representations of birds and animals, or scenes from hunting and gladiatorial combats. In the fourth century Christian motifs begin to appear; a recent Dorsetshire discovery shows the figure of Christ himself. In the dining-room, which was normally the main feature of the house, the diners' couches were placed outside the margins of the mosaic which adorned the floor.

This and other important parts of the house were often warmed by the hypocaust method: air heated by an external furnace was introduced from below and brought up ducts hidden behind the plaster of the walls. Neither the even temperature of the rooms nor the hot baths, readily available in a separate bath-house, nor many of the minor amenities and artistic embellishments of villa life were to be matched in any part of Britain for many long centuries, once the Roman presence had been withdrawn.

Decline and Fall

The primary reasons for the overthrow of Roman Britain are to be sought in the decay of the western Roman empire as a whole and its loss of the power to grapple effectively with the barbarian world beyond the frontiers. In the third century, the condition of Britain seems to have been in general more tranquil and orderly than that of many other provinces: it may be noticed in passing that this was when the Christian religion began to gather adherents here and probably had its first martyrs, though the earliest mention of British bishops and theological disputants is not until 314. But towards the close of the third century a new system of coastal defences had to be established, significantly named the forts of the 'Saxon Shore'. Round the coast from Norfolk to the Isle of Wight, and to a smaller extent in the west as well, new earthworks and town defences were set up, behind which mixed garrisons of soldiers and sailors were held in readiness to repel raiders. For another two generations, however, the civil zone at least had nothing worse to fear than occasional raids, though these came from Ireland as well as across the North Sea. Then, in 367, a synchronized attack by Saxons, Picts of the far north, and Scots from Ireland overran the Wall and plundered a large part of the province. Control was eventually re-established, the Wall rebuilt, and the coastal defence scheme extended up into Yorkshire. But it seems likely that the garrisoning of the Wall was now replaced by reliance upon self-governing tribes of 'friendly natives', who were to hold the Picts at bay beyond the Forth. The power of Rome was shrinking.

Contemporaries, of course, did not see it so clearly. In the fourth century the towns naturally spent more of their money on new fortifications than on other types of public building, and they were perhaps frequented to a decreasing extent by affluent Celts of the upper class. But there is no clear evidence that the number of petty tradesmen and artisans within their walls was seriously on the decline. As for the villa population, the presence of coins proves that many sites were still occupied in the last decades of the century, even as far north as east Yorkshire, and in areas more remote from attack the buildings show continuing prosperity. Lydney, for instance, on the north side of the Severn estuary was then the goal of many pilgrimages, directed to a new shrine of the Celtic hunting and water god, Nodens. The revival of paganism, a generation after Constantine had made Christianity the official religion of the empire, might be a reaction to disturbed conditions. But the lavish character of the buildings and offerings found at Lydney points clearly to a state of affairs in which wealthy devotees were not afraid to travel.

But the province could not survive the withdrawal of its garrison, which began with the seduction of some of the troops by pretenders to the imperial throne and was continued through the official recall of others for service nearer the heart of the empire. By 410 the central administration had likewise disappeared, and in that year the emperor of the west sent instructions to the cantonal authorities to organize their own defence. He was writing in the year when Rome itself fell to the Goths. Since what was intended as a temporary expedient was not followed by any effective long-term resumption of Roman control over the island, this date best marks the close of the epoch in which Britain had been firmly attached to the Mediterranean world and ruled from far-away Rome.

The Legacy of Roman Rule

Since Roman rule had lasted for a period as long as that which separates ourselves from the age of Shakespeare, it is reasonable to ask, What was its legacy? As regards the make-up of the population, it was an occupation which left little trace behind it. The climate did not encourage many administrators or wealthy merchants from across the Channel to make permanent homes here; even the time-expired veterans of the multi-national armies, who must often have settled down with native wives, were too few to have any marked effect upon the Celts. But the Welsh language shows that the Celts had borrowed many words, as we might expect, from their conquerors, though few, apparently, in the realms of politics and law. English took over only the Latin of certain place-names, adapted no doubt from their Celtic forms. Lincoln, for instance, includes *colonia*, and Portsmouth *portus*, meaning 'harbour'; but the most numerous and significant are the endings in 'chester' or 'cester', from *castra*, 'fort', and those in 'street', from *via strata*, 'a paved road'.

The revived use of many Roman town sites was certainly an important factor in the later development of the island. London, York, Canterbury, and Winchester all owed some of their special prestige to their association with the period of Roman rule, and in many other cases the Roman choice of a site stimulated later growth because it had become a nodal point in their road system. For the roads, too, played a big part when traffic revived, having been so strongly built that they could survive centuries of disuse and misuse. Altogether, the fact that Britain had been a Roman province and preserved these evidences of its past status does something to explain the early date at which the English, as compared with other Germanic peoples, achieved the unification of their new possessions.

So much for the long-term influence of the Roman occupation on the future making of England. In the havoc of the fifth and sixth centuries, however, what was most important was the handing-on of the Christian faith. In the arts, the Celts swept aside the stereotyped and conventional work of the Roman period, and there was a second efflorescence of the freer styles of their distant past. But in religion the seed sown in the last Roman centuries bore fruit in the missionary church of Wales, the completion of the conversion of Ireland, and the sixth-century 'age of the saints.'

3

THE COMING OF THE ENGLISH

THE fifth and sixth centuries of the Christian era are a dark period
in the history of western Europe, when the well-ordered Roman
world was falling to pieces and barbarian tribes staked out rival
claims to the inheritance. To us looking back the age appears
all the darker because one aspect of the cultural decline is a dearth
of written records. The best that still continued were ecclesiastical,
but 455 was the last year when the British Church was certainly in
touch with the continent. The island itself has no literature from
the fifth century; from the sixth, nothing but a single rhetorical
account of its fate in a kind of sermon preached by a British monk,
Gildas, *On the Downfall and Conquest of Britain*. The first description of the English conquest from the English side was written
more than a hundred years after the main events were completed,
in the *Ecclesiastical History* of the Venerable Bede. The archaeo-
logical evidence is scanty and often open to different intepretations,
though the identification of pre-Christian graveyards gives us one of
the main clues to the pattern of early Anglo-Saxon settlement.

When Britain ceased to be administered regularly as a province
of the Roman empire, its people were exposed to dangers which
were neither completely new nor completely overwhelming. As
we have seen, attacks from the far north and from overseas had
been going on for a long time, and there is some reason to believe
that Saxons had already been brought in at some points in the east
as a means of strengthening the garrison. To grapple with these
problems the people of each canton were left with a romanized
local government; the most prominent towns, too, had their local
administrations. These bodies had numerous fortifications at their
disposal, if there was sufficient determination and organizing
capacity left to keep them manned. But determination and
organizing capacity appear to have been forthcoming chiefly in

the former military zone of the north and west, where Highland
Picts and the Scots from Ireland were held successfully at bay.
What had been the civil zone in the south and east was less well
defended, chiefly perhaps because a more civilized life had made
its population less apt for war.

The Anglo-Saxon Invaders

Our forefathers, the people on the other side of the North
Sea who were later to turn the lowland zone into England, accordingly found a greater ease and doubtless additional zest in their
old trade of plundering: the 18-lb silver dish and spoons, which
were buried for safety at Mildenhall in Suffolk (and found again
in 1940), show the kind of thing they were after. Perhaps some
plunderers were then hired by the British authorities to keep out
other plunderers, but attempted settlement was in any case the
natural sequel to the period of hit-and-run raids. Bede gives a clear
picture of a final stage in something like a mass migration.

> Those who came over belonged to three of the very formidable
> races of Germany – Saxons, Angles, and Jutes. From the Jutes
> are descended the people of Kent and the Isle of Wight, and
> those in the province of Wessex opposite the Isle of Wight who
> are called Jutes to this day. From the Saxons, that is, the
> country now called Old Saxony, came the East, South, and West
> Saxons. And from the Angles – the country of 'Angulus', which
> lies between the provinces of the Jutes and Saxons and remains
> unpopulated to this day – are descended the East and Middle
> Angles, the Mercians, all the Northumbrians, who live north of
> the River Humber, and other English peoples.

But the picture is altogether too precise. The modern view is
that the English of the future came from the whole of the coastline
between the mouths of the Rhine and Schleswig – possibly also
from the south of Sweden – and that the Frisians in particular
formed a big enough element to deserve separate mention. They
are the people whose name survives in the modern Frisian
Islands, and were at this time the leading seafarers of the North
Sea area. The English came, moreover, in a less highly organized

fashion than Bede implies, with raids and forays into the hinterland preparing the way for settlers' expeditions, mostly quite small, in which families and household gear were ferried over. Kent may, indeed, have been seized by a mainly Jutish mercenary force, invited in to garrison Thanet. But elsewhere many successive parties must have made their way independently up the rivers, attacking, retreating, and attacking again, until eventually a foothold was won.

The kind of ships they employed can be judged from a specimen excavated from a peat bog at Nydam in Schleswig (from which the Angles came), and from the imprints left in the ground by the vanished timbers of a second vessel, used for a ship-burial at Sutton Hoo in Suffolk: they were probably built in about 400 and 625 respectively, so they span the period of the conquest. Both craft were long and narrow: that at Nydam was 77 × 11 feet, the Sutton Hoo ship a little larger. The hulls were clinker-built, that is, of overlapping planks, and the sides so low amidships that high seas must often have washed over them. They had no sail and were propelled by 28 and 38 oars respectively, with a primitive form of rowlock which prevented a reversal of direction. In the absence of a proper keel, they cannot have been very stable, and there was no deck; even the steersman, straining at his board in the stern, had only a bracer to steady his feet. It was from rowing-boats like these that Saxon war-bands, drenched to the skin, descended upon the shores of Britain.

It is possible to describe their appearance. The Schleswig peat bogs have even preserved from the invasion period the clothes of a dead man, folded beside the body. From a slightly later time we have a Northumbrian whalebone casket, on which figures of fighting-men are carved. They wore long-sleeved woven tunics, combined either with a kilt-like garment and puttees to cover the legs, or with long woollen trousers tapering down to the feet and supported by a belt. On top, they wore a large woollen cloak, about two yards square, fastened at the shoulder. When the kilt was included, they must have looked rather like the Scottish Highlanders of later days.

The most common weapon of the Saxons was the spear, with its shaft of ash-wood and a length of about ten feet. They also had five-foot bows, shooting iron- or bone-headed arrows. In some cases the shafts of the arrows were notched, perhaps so that the owners could find them again in the corpses of their enemies and boast of their successes in the after-battle feasting. Iron swords and round wooden shields were used. The latter were covered with hides and sometimes embellished with metal ornament; a very fine specimen was buried in the Sutton Hoo ship, alongside the king who once bore it in battle.

The Course of the Invasion

As has already been indicated, very little indeed is known about the course of the long warfare between the heathen Saxon and the Celt. It probably began with a series of successful incursions against spasmodic British resistance, in which Saxon arms were carried far across the country. There is good evidence that this was followed by a period of British counter-attacks, including an important victory over the invaders, gained somewhere about the year 500 at 'Mons Badonicus', which may conceivably be the same place as Badbury Rings in Dorsetshire. It is possible that the British military leader at this time was the figure transformed by later legend into 'King Arthur'; some scholars have even seen in his 'knights of the round table' a dim recollection of a force of cavalry, such as a romanized Briton might have introduced for routing the Saxon footmen. Continental sources suggest that a part of the immigrant population actually fled back overseas.

However that may be, it is certain that by about the middle of the sixth century the tide of battle turned again, and by its close Saxon military power had extended its hold from the south and east into the west, the midlands, and the north. Conversely, the British kingdoms – to be considered later in the chapter – had ceased to rule outside Devon and Cornwall, Wales, north-west England, and the Scotland of the future.

We may now turn from the obscure military history of the conquest to the great social and economic event which accompanied it, namely the advance of the frontier of Anglo-Saxon settlement. The two processes did not necessarily have the same pace. Where the existing British population was thinly spread and much vacant ground available for cultivation, some Saxon settlement may have preceded the winning of military control. On the other hand, a Saxon victory in a particular district would not necessarily be followed at once by the arrival of numerous settlers. Thus the growth of England was a rather haphazard process, about which only one generalization is possible, namely that over a large part of the country a new society completely replaced the old.

It is impossible to say what proportion of Britons the Saxons exterminated, what proportion they drove back into the west, and what proportion they retained as slaves – or left under freer conditions in isolated enclaves. But it seems clear that, if the newcomers had commonly had British women for wives or British men working alongside them in the fields, Celtic words would have been introduced into English speech in connection with the running of the house and the agricultural routine. Broadly speaking, they were not: even the Celtic river names, already mentioned, survive less frequently in the east than in the west. As for placenames, those of Celtic origin are negligible as far west as Worcestershire and are fewer than one per cent of the total even in the late-conquered county of Devon. The evidence of language is confirmed by that of institutions. As a general rule the Saxons did not even take over such local religious cults as had survived the coming of Christianity to the Celtic peoples, and their systems of law, agriculture, and social relations remained solidly based upon Germanic foundations.

The tide of Anglo-Saxon settlement, one of the most important movements in the whole history of the island, flowed roughly as follows. Three main coastal areas, each connected with an important river system, provided the convenient points of entry. Kent and south Sussex were permanently occupied from a very early date, while the lower Thames valley was the route by which the early kingdoms of Middlesex (which probably included Surrey and Hertfordshire) and Essex received their population. The second area concerned was the fenland, which gave access both to East Anglia and to a Middle Anglia, represented by the modern counties of Cambridge, Huntingdon, and Northampton. In the third place, the Humber estuary led the way to Lindsey, still the name of the northernmost of the three Parts of Lincolnshire, and into east Yorkshire, where the kingdom of Deira was established. These regions formed the nucleus of England.

Other regions were settled, on the whole, at a considerably later date. Since they were also less easily accessible to immigrants from overseas and lay closer to the mountain districts where the Celts had their main strength, it is reasonable to suppose that they were less completely anglicized. In the upper Thames valley, for instance, the Saxons appear to have been overrun by the Celts for a considerable time before they were able to resume the advance to the Severn and the south-west, out of which the kingdom of Wessex eventually grew. Some intermixture may also have taken place during the occupation of the valley of the Trent, which made the midlands into a kind of march along the Welsh border, where later the kingdom of Mercia was to be established. In the north the new kingdom of Bernicia began with widely scattered settlements in Northumberland and Durham, while the strength of the Britons is attested by the long survival of their little kingdom of Elmet, on the east side of the Pennines in the neighbourhood of modern Leeds.

The New Settlements

Such were the stages by which the English, as the sixth century drew to its close, had succeeded in staking out their claim to the civil zone of the old Roman province. But they had staked it out in a very different way from the method used to create its earlier pattern. This is true both of town and country.

Gildas wrote of the destruction of the twenty-eight Roman towns, and it seems to be broadly true that those which did not perish in the Saxon search for plunder crumbled slowly away as their usefulness and the people who used them gradually disappeared. Where the site was convenient for habitation, it may never have been entirely deserted, although the urban institutions and way of life had vanished. Canterbury, for instance, while ceasing to be the Roman *Durovernum*, had some continuous history, probably as a kind of tribal headquarters. London and a few other ports must also have kept up some activity, because the immigrants did not deliberately cut themselves off from their homelands on the continent. There was at least a trickle of trade, to which the Jutes of Kent were partly indebted for a higher level of culture than other parts of heathen England. Nevertheless, it seems to be significant of the English attitude that, even when they settled in the vicinity of a Roman town, they often preferred to settle near, rather than on, the Roman site: Verulamium, for example, gave way to St Albans, placed on the hill outside the Roman walls and at a distance from the great Roman thorough-fare which the Saxons called the Watling Street. The ruins of Rome's handiwork, still standing high, may well have seemed to them supernatural, though it was a poet's fancy which called them 'cities visible from afar, the cunning work of giants, the wondrous fortifications in stone which are on this earth'.

The Saxon pattern of rural settlement was almost equally a new departure. So little use was made of the Roman villa system that not a single name was handed on by its later occupants. It is impossible to say that the estate of which a particular villa was the centre never continued as an agricultural unit, for common sense argues that the fields would be taken over when they suited the tillage plans of the newcomers. The same must be true of the less easily identifiable lands of the Celtic farmsteads. But the broad picture is that of a new people choosing to occupy new land in a new way: the names of the English villages of today show what locations they chose and how they developed them.

The English very largely ignored the main areas of earlier settlement, scattered on the chalk hillsides of the southern counties, in favour of gravel soils in the river valleys, where heavier crops could be grown: for in their old homes on the continent they had been agriculturists rather than stock-keepers. Their selection of sites can be roughly traced across the map. Place-names which originally terminated in *inga* mark the very early period, when groups were carving out territory for themselves under a definite leader, since this ending indicates that it is the settlement of his family or dependants: thus Reading signifies 'Red's people'. Such names are particularly frequent in Sussex and Essex. Another ending which occurs more often in the east of England than in the west is *ham*, meaning 'homestead'. A still more common ending, which became widespread at a rather later date, is *ton*: this originally meant 'enclosure', but quickly became the regular word for 'village'. Thus Luton signifies 'village on the river Lea'. In the use of the ending -*den*, on the other hand, we have an early indication of subsidiary settlements, formed when people moved out to live in what had formerly been recognized as areas for grazing pigs. Thus Tenterden signifies 'the swine pasture of the Thanet people'. Within limits, therefore, the pertinacious map-reader can trace the way in which the newcomers began the settlement of a particular district of England in accordance with the way of life they brought with them from the continent.

Wherever possible, they grouped their homes in closely formed villages. In the early days a rough wooden stockade would be erected for protection. Inside it, we may picture a collection of huts, built from wood or wattle-and-daub and steeply roofed with thatch. Outside lay the fields which the ox-teams ploughed. Over all, the smell of wood smoke and the sight of it lying in layers in the valley mists. Behind the narrow, guarded gateway in the stockade there were barns and outhouses for cattle and gear. But certainly the largest and most important building would normally be the hall, constructed in wood in much the same way as the big barns of later days.

On one of the long sides of the hall the lord and his wife had their seats, while the guests of honour were placed opposite them, near the blazing log fire in the centre, whose smoke billowed among the rafters and only slowly found its way out through an uncovered opening in the roof. Here there would be feasting on occasion, when the long drinking-horns of the great and the rough pots used by ordinary men were alike filled with strong ale, and the songs of the minstrel drew on memories of their German past. And always the spears and shields hung in readiness round the walls of the hall, for at any time the guard might come running from the gate to warn of enemies emerging from the forest bypaths.

Agriculture, Law, and Religion

Life was not all feasting or fighting, however: it was mainly farming. Of the details at this early period we have very little direct knowledge. Barley, oats, rye, and flax were grown, as well as much-prized wheat; probably more of barley than the other grains, because it provided both food and drink. It is thought that the fields were already of the large 'open' type, where each co-worker perhaps received his strip of the arable in proportion to his contribution to the plough-team. There must also have been careful use made of all the rest of the ground that had been cleared or otherwise brought under control, so as to secure enough fodder to keep the plough oxen and a few riding-horses alive through the winter, to say nothing of the sheep, dairy cattle, and pigs essential to a community which had to be prepared to supply nearly all its own needs.

Each small kingdom was no doubt knit together to some extent by a little internal trade: grindstones and salt, for instance, could not always be procured locally, and the absence of a coinage did not altogether prevent long-distance sales by barter. But the kingdom was essentially a region governed by certain laws and customs. An innocent man could clear himself of most charges by his own oath and the oaths of his friends. But where death by violence was involved, as it very often was, in the absence of any police force it was the duty of the family to avenge a murder. This could be done by means of a blood-feud, but instead of its terminating when the original wrong had been punished, the result was likely to be a vendetta continuing from generation to generation. Accordingly, an important aspect of early law, to which the Christian Church later gave active support, was the provision of a tariff of compensation for the eventuality of violent death. Every man had his *wergild* or 'man-price', which his family could claim from the man who killed him and from that man's family. Some men were legally of greater value than others. In Kentish law, for example, the wergild of a free man was 100 shillings, that of a noble three times as great.

But no law had a greater binding-power than the obligation of loyalty to a lord. From the lord might come all that was best in life: protection against enemies, feast and carousal, perhaps the gift of the land a man held, and certainly the warmth of comradeship in the day of battle. If the lord were struck down, there was no greater shame than to survive him: he must be followed into the next world – if next world there was.

Though the names of the chief Saxon gods are enshrined in our days of the week – the Tiw of Tuesday, Woden of Wednesday, Thunor of Thursday, and Frig of Friday – their religion seems to have been a rather shadowy thing. Woden, the god of war, was the leading divinity, from whom most of the Saxon dynasties claimed descent. A goddess of the spring season, Eostra, has given us our word for Easter. Yule, too, comes from the twelve-day Saxon feast at mid-winter, when men dressed up in animal skins and offered sacrifices for good luck in the coming year. Many such seasonal observations, together with their ways of placating the monsters and fairies whose presence they detected in wood and stream and hill, went back to the remotest past of their ancestors on the continent.

How strongly these beliefs were held was put to the test in 597, when the landing of Augustine in Kent opened a new chapter in the history of the English. But we must first consider what the two dark centuries had meant for other parts of the island, where Christianity had not been extinguished by chaos.

Celtic Kingdoms and Churches

It has already been pointed out that the Britons of the highland zone offered a more effective resistance to attack, and their position was no doubt strengthened by some addition to their population from areas of Saxon raids and settlements. The fifth century therefore saw the establishment of a line of British kingdoms stretching from the Firth of Forth to the south-western peninsula. In the north they covered the whole width of the island, and the southern border of Strathclyde, whose capital lay at Dumbarton on the north bank of the Clyde estuary, reached as far as Cumbria, which in turn stretched down to Wales. The Welsh kingdoms likewise linked up with 'West Wales', which lay south of the Bristol Channel. If their rulers had not been increasingly distracted by feuds against each other, such as the early poetry of Wales describes, the long struggle with the English might have ended in a different division of the island. As it was, by the close of the sixth century their confederacies against the English had lost most of their vigour, with the result that the latter had reached the Severn, were approaching the Dee, and were beginning to move up towards the Firth of Forth. Though Cumbria or Cumberland means 'the land of the Cymry' (or Welsh), north-west England and, to a lesser extent, south-east Scotland were fated to lose in the long run the stamp of the Celtic kingdoms to which they once belonged.

But for a time the whole of this continuous area was the home of a Celtic Christian culture to which the heathen English had no parallel. The region possessed a bardic poetry, on which the earliest surviving Welsh literature is based. It also has a direct literary memorial in the inscriptions to be found on widely scattered stone crosses and other stone monuments, some of which are exquisitely sculptured. The lettering, which consists chiefly of names, is partly in Latin and partly in a Celtic alphabet, known as 'ogham'; the latter group are the oldest Christian monument inscriptions in a native language which survive from any former province of the Roman empire. The most striking common feature of the region, however, was the spread of an austere form of the monastic life, which had already travelled from its first home in the Egyptian desert as far as the coastal islands off France and Spain.

In the Celtic Church the 'age of the saints' refers in the first place to the devotees and visionaries who set out to worship God in solitude, making their homes in circumstances of extreme hardship on islands and uninhabited peninsulas all round the coasts of Britain, from the Scillies and Caldy to North Rona and the Brough of Deerness in the Orkneys. But the presence of one saint attracted others, so that a community often became established under an abbot and monastic Rule, whose members lived partly in retirement and partly as mission priests among the neighbouring population. Such a place was Bardsey Island in Caernarvonshire, claimed as 'the burial-place of twenty thousand saints', and there came to be many mainland foundations, as at Glastonbury and Tintagel. It was this type of church organization, too, that the British-born Patrick carried across to Ireland, the conversion of which was completed before his death in 461. From there, almost exactly a century later, Columba carried it back across the sea to Iona, in the Inner Hebrides.

Cornwall and Wales; Origins of Scotland

The secular history of the kingdom based on Cornwall is chiefly remarkable for the transplantation of population which gave Brittany its name and language; this movement of some of the Celts overseas, which has been termed the first British colonial venture, seems to have been occasioned, not by any Saxon pressure but by the inroads of the Irish. The type of pottery in use in Cornwall shows that the Cornish trade with the Mediterranean, including

Plates 5 and 6. *The amphitheatre at Caerleon, Monmouthshire.* Here the troops of the second (Augusta) legion, based on Caerleon fort, were trained and amused. Wooden seats for the whole legion (a nominal 6,000) ran round the earthen banks which provided the core of the building. Only the backing walls, passages and entrances (eight of them), were built of stone. It has been excavated and is accounted the finest example of an amphitheatre in Britain. (Cf. text p. 17.)

Plate 7. *The Nydam Ship.* Excavated in 1863, this is now in the Schleswig-Holstein Museum of Pre-history. Note the lowness amidships and the lack of a proper keel – no more than a continuation of the stem and stern-posts of the ship. The rowing speed probably varied between five and three knots, according to whether it carried unencumbered war-bands or was crowded with settlers. (Cf. text p. 31.)

Plate 8. *Barn interior at Harmondsworth, Middlesex.* From the Saxon epic-poem *Beowulf* it is clear that the Saxon hall was a timber-framed building, 'tall and wide-gabled', where the warriors slept and 'clear voiced poets' sang at the feastings. Bede speaks of 'a great fire in the middle of the room' and of the roof 'being made of wattles and thatch'. Barns in England and north Germany are constructed on closely similar lines; and, in such a traditional sort of building, it is likely that they descend directly from Saxon forms. In such a barn as this, we probably reach as near as is possible to the interior of a Saxon hall. (See M. and C.H.B. Quennell, *Everyday Life in Anglo-Saxon, Viking and Norman Times,* pp. 18–27.) (Cf. text p. 36.)

Plate 9. *The Lindisfarne Gospels.* This is the start of St. Matthew's Gospel in the Vulgate text. It reads: 'Liber generationis Jesu Christi, filii David, filii Abraham'. (Cf. text p. 50.)

Plate 10. *The Ruthwell Cross, Dumfriesshire.* Early 8th century: it is 18 feet high, with the upper part restored and replaced the wrong way round. The two lowest reliefs show Christ with Mary Magdalene (upper) and Christ healing the blind man – both surrounded by Latin characters. The runic passages from the 'Dream of the Rood' are on the two narrower sides (for this great Saxon poem see M. Alexander, *The Earliest English Poems* (Penguin), pp. 103–109). (Cf. text pp. 48 and 51.)

Plates 7 and 8

Plate 9

Plate 10

perhaps the exportation of tin, continued at a time when the rest of the island had little or no long-distance commerce. Cornwall kept its independence until the ninth century, and its language, akin to Welsh, did not begin to give place to English until the Reformation. Some Celtic words are still retained in west Cornwall, and as for names –

> By Pol, Tre, and Pen
> You may know the Cornishmen.

The Welsh, on account of their central position in the Irish Sea, had always to face west as well as east. In the fifth century their great achievement was the repulsion of the Irish, who before the end of the Roman period had established a hold on Pembrokeshire and the west of Caernarvonshire. According to tradition, they were driven out by a prince who migrated to Wales with eight sons from the region of the Forth; he was regarded as the founder of several dynasties in the north and west of the country. Be that as it may, Wales did become a mosaic of tiny kingdoms, with ruling families which in some cases preserved their identities through eight centuries. What they ruled over was invariably a simple pastoral form of society, in which the most important class were the free tribesmen, rather like the members of a Scottish clan. They lived at a distance from one another, especially in summer, when they took the cattle, their main source of wealth, to the hill pasture or *hafod*. Beneath them there was an unfree class, which lived in villages, tilled the soil, and paid tribute from its crops. A scattered and disunited people could not defend for ever the long frontier towards England, and much of the poetry which, together with music, became a national heritage of the Welsh, records the gradual encroachments. Thus a ninth-century poem laments the loss of Shrewsbury by the princes of Powys, who had left only a sister to mourn for them:

> Wandering Heledd am I called.
> O God, to whom are given
> The lands of my brothers and their steeds?
> I look down from Wrekin Fort
> On the land of Freuer.
> Longing for the land of my brothers breaks my heart.

The origins of the later kingdom of Scotland are more complex than those of Wales, but by 600 north Britain, too, was struggling towards a separate identity. The main elements in the south of the country have already been indicated – Strathclyde, the smaller British kingdoms east of it, and the Saxon kingdom of Bernicia beginning to move up the east coast at their expense. But Strathclyde had other neighbours to the north of the Forth–Clyde line, whom Rome had never tamed and to whom Christianity was largely unknown.

These principal inhabitants of the Scottish Highlands, whom Latin writers called *Picti*, had figured prominently as assailants of the Roman province. At that time they were already skilful builders of small castles, the drystone round towers called 'brochs'; but virtually nothing is known of their then way of life and, as their language had never been deciphered, it is not even clear how far their origins were Celtic. But by the fifth century the Picts had two powerful kingdoms, often at war with each other, which were based respectively on Inverness-shire and the northern islands and on the rich valley of the Tay. From this period onwards they developed an astonishing symbolic art, with both geometrical and animal designs, incised at first on unshaped boulders and later sculptured on dressed slabs in relief. Since the ogham inscriptions, which accompany some of these later works, cannot be read, the symbols remain unexplained, but the skill of the execution leaves no doubt that the Picts had reached a high level of technical as well as of purely artistic achievement.

Meanwhile, however, the first small inroads upon their territory had been made in Argyll, where the little kingdom of Dalriada was set up by the Scots, a tribe which already dominated the adjacent north-east corner of Ireland. Here Columba came with twelve companions in 563, to found his monastery on Iona. A member of the reigning family among the Irish, he was both statesman and saint; his influence resulted both in the conversion of the northern Picts and in the confirmation of the work begun among the southern Picts by earlier missionaries from Strathclyde. Thus the remote island of Iona, where Columba died in 597, gave Scotland a religious capital long before it had any political one. Iona was also destined to be one of the main sources of the Christianity which was now to reshape the England of the heathen kings.

4

THE CONVERSION OF ENGLAND

THE landing of Augustine and his company of nearly forty on the coast of Thanet shortly before Easter Day, 597, began the process by which England renewed its ties with Mediterranean civilization, ties which were not to be broken again until the Reformation. The Latin language, more advanced political ideas, and many arts and sciences followed in the wake of the Church, as first the kings and then the peoples of the little English kingdoms, one by one and with temporary lapses into heathenism, came to accept the Christian faith. In the eyes of Pope Gregory the Great, who had sent Augustine to the island, the Anglian boys he had noticed in the slave market at Rome represented a call to save pagan souls from imminent danger of hell-fire. But at the same time Roman tradition required that their conversion should be based upon the orderly foundations of bishops' sees and a well organized relationship between bishop and king, so that the Church as by-law established might also play a leading part in secular society.

The king of Kent was already married to a Frankish Christian princess, who had her own chaplain and church at Canterbury, and the kingdom (as we have already seen) had close commercial links across the narrow seas. The conversion of the king and many of his people, and the establishment of Augustine's see at Canterbury, were therefore quickly accomplished. Yet the initial impetus was soon lost. The Welsh Church refused either to accept Gregory's imposition of Augustine as their archbishop or in any way to assist his mission in converting the heathen who had usurped possession of so much of the island. From Kent an advance was made into the little kingdom of Essex, which at that time included London; but the bishop of London was ejected and the kingdom relapsed into paganism for nearly forty years. In East Anglia, two

Christian rulers left no lasting impression on their subjects, and even in Kent heathen idols were still allowed their adherents.

So much for the south-east. But Augustine and his immediate successors as archbishop faced a situation in which the leadership among the English kingdoms was passing from Kent to Northumbria, a new state formed by the union of Deira and Bernicia and strengthened by victory over the British. A mission under Paulinus therefore accompanied a Kentish royal bride to Northumbria, where Bede's *History* gives us our first glimpse of an English king in consultation with his council of wise men or Witan, a famous scene in which their exposure of the emptiness of the religion of Woden is made to precede Edwin's decision to receive baptism.

The soul of man [says one councillor] is like a sparrow, which on a dark and rainy night passes for a moment through the door of a king's hall. Entering, it is for the moment surrounded by light and warmth and safe from the wintry storm; but after a short spell of brightness and quiet, it vanishes through another door into the dark storm from which it came. Likewise the life of man is for a moment visible; but what went before or is to come remains unknown. If therefore this new doctrine can tell us something about these mysteries, by all means let us follow it.

But the life of the king was also transitory: seven years after his baptism on Easter Day, 627, Edwin was killed in battle against the British and their heathen allies, after which only a single missionary dared to remain in the partly christianized northern kingdom.

The Celtic Mission

In 635, however, a second mission entered England, this time across the moors of the north, from Iona instead of Rome, and with the religious ideas and methods that had grown up in the isolated churches of the Celtic west. This mission had the strong support of a new king of Northumbria, who had won the throne as a Christian convert returning from exile at Iona. Indeed, its leader, Aidan, established his monastic community close by the royal fortress of Bamburgh, on the wind-swept tidal island of

Lindisfarne. His companions were volunteers and enthusiasts, who travelled the country sharing the hardships of the common people to whom they ministered. After penetrating the whole of the big northern kingdom, at mid-century the mission spread into Mercia and carried the gospel for the third time to Essex.

Meanwhile the Papacy, which had given the Canterbury mission every encouragement, sent a bishop from Gaul who began work in Wessex, and a Burgundian under the direct control of the see of Canterbury finally achieved the conversion of East Anglia. Thus after two-thirds of a century nearly all the kingdoms were officially Christian, but it was a Christianity based half upon Rome and Canterbury and half upon Iona and Lindisfarne. This meant a rivalry between missions, which was more than a question of prestige.

During their long period of isolation the Celtic Churches had acquired, alongside their more loosely knit organization and the great reputation for humility and self-denial won by their leaders, some peculiarities of custom. A difference in tonsure gave them a long-haired clergy, which was inconvenient in an age when it was desirable for a clergyman to be instantly recognizable as such. Difficulty also arose from the fact that, under the Celtic system, the abbot of a monastery had more authority than the bishop of a diocese. But the most important difference was in the method used to calculate the date of Easter, which meant a clash in the observance of the most sacred of ecclesiastical festivals. If England continued to recognize these divergent practices, she would lose part of the benefit of her new cultural link with the Mediterranean world and all the unifying effect of a Church organization which went beyond the separate bounds of the little English kingdoms. It was therefore a landmark in our history when in 663, at a synod held in the abbey at Whitby, the king of Northumbria transferred his spiritual allegiance from near-by Iona to distant Rome.

Some dissentient clergy retired to Ireland, but the main result of the synod was the additional strength conferred upon the archbishopric of Canterbury as the link with Rome. Within two decades the conversion of England was completed by a successful mission to Sussex, isolated by the Weald, and to the Isle of Wight. Even before this, the work of the bishops in all parts of the country had been systematized by a new archbishop, a Greek known as Theodore of Tarsus, who came to England as the direct nominee of the Pope. Arriving in a strange land at the age of 67, this remarkable man gave it more than twenty years of vigorous service. By the time of his death, every diocese had been brought firmly under his control, while the great school which he founded at Canterbury exercised an influence as far away as Ireland. Thus Church unity long preceded national unity.

Cultural Level of Seventh-Century England

Before considering in more detail the impact of the Church upon the life of the people, we may note that this life was no longer altogether barbaric. So far as we can tell, the settlements in England were made at the outset by peoples at a low level of culture with the single exception of the Jutes of Kent, whose jewellers and goldsmiths were amazingly skilful. But the ship burial at Sutton Hoo, which is believed to date from about the period of the synod of Whitby, shows that by then great accumulations of wealth had become possible. The ship was used for a cenotaph, raised presumably in honour of a king of East Anglia, a relatively small state which was helped to preserve its identity by the landward barrier of the fens. We cannot say for certain which king or whether he was a Christian, though the placing of items with Christian associations in the space where the body would have lain is a strong argument for thinking so.

What the burial shows clearly is that East Anglian craftsmen were capable of astonishingly delicate and elaborate workmanship in metal and enamel inlay, that gold was readily available for what appear to be regalia, and that battle equipment might extend beyond arms and armour to a wrought-iron standard, spiked for treading into the ground and topped by a bronze emblem such as the Roman legions had once employed. The quantity of the grave-goods, which include twenty-six items of gold jewellery and sixteen pieces of late-classical silver, is no less remarkable than the quality. It suggests that trade across the North Sea, combined perhaps with the profits of piracy, must have been a regular source of wealth to East Anglia and presumably also to other kingdoms. We can only make guesses as to the history of a 27½-inch ornamented silver salver, bearing the stamp of official Byzantine assayers, which after a century and a half had come to rest at Sutton Hoo. A collection of thirty-seven Merovingian gold coins, on the other hand, confirms other indications that the English kingdoms traded extensively with the Franks, while the fact that several articles appear to have been made in Sweden or at least by Swedes points fairly clearly to connections farther afield. It has even been suggested that the East Anglian royal house, whose origins are unknown, may have been of Swedish descent.

Church Organization

Whether Swedes or Saxons, kings were separated by a wide gulf from ordinary men. Therefore it is not surprising that, in almost every one of the English kingdoms, the conversion began with the baptism of the main ruler: Mercia provides the big exception, and even there the presence of a missionary was only tolerated after a marriage alliance had led to the baptism of an under-king. But the English kings did not usually force their subjects to follow the royal example. Instead, the initiative rested with the missionaries who, travelling under royal protection, expounded the new faith and called upon their hearers to be baptized. At Yeavering in the foothills of the Cheviots, for instance, we are told that Paulinus was baptizing in the river Glen for thirty-six days on end. At the other end of the Northumbrian kingdom an old man cherished the memory, which was faithfully passed on to Bede, of how

> he himself had been baptized at noon-day, by Bishop Paulinus, in the presence of King Edwin, and with him a great multitude of the people, in the river Trent . . . And he was also wont to describe the person of the same Paulinus, saying that he was tall of stature, stooping somewhat, his hair black, his visage thin, his nose slender and aquiline, his aspect both venerable and awe-inspiring.

The Celtic missionaries were perhaps less awe-inspiring in their appearance than Roman Paulinus, but the extreme poverty in which they chose to live brought them closer to their hearers, and their generosity in sharing what little they had, about which there are many stories, showed that they practised the love they preached.

The sites of some parish churches may still mark the spot where the first itinerant preacher set up a rough wooden cross as the first step in his mission to that neighbourhood. The north of England and, to a lesser extent, other parts began to be enriched soon after the conversion by the erection of beautifully carved stone crosses, such as survive to the present day at Bewcastle and Ruthwell; it is tempting to suppose that these treasured parochial possessions replaced an older cross of wood. Be that as it may, a big gap had somehow to be bridged between the creation of a body of Christians in a place and the establishment of a parish there.

At first, there were only sufficient clergy to form the household or personal following of the bishop, who sent them out on various missionary tasks throughout his diocese. Then came a stage when a few collegiate churches or 'minsters' were built, each containing a body of clergy who served the surrounding area. Lastly, parishes were brought gradually into existence, as and when a local lord or thegn[1] found that his piety or his dignity impelled him to provide his own estate with a separate church and priest. These first parish churches have for the most part vanished without trace, since the building was a little wooden structure, which easily perished or was easily outgrown, and the decision to erect it on the thegn's private land did not need to be recorded by charter.[2] As for the first parish priests, all that is known of them is that they came from the class of free peasants; received their religious instruction from the bishop; were endowed by the thegn with a portion of land, called the 'glebe', which they tilled themselves; and eked out a living from church dues and fees.

The diocese was the unit of fundamental importance, both for the establishment of Christianity within each kingdom and for binding the kingdoms together into a single ecclesiastical whole. Pope Gregory had originally intended that the island should have two archbishops, each ruling over twelve bishops, but the arch-

[1] See p. 60
[2] See p. 53

bishopric of York was not set up until the eighth century and never received its full allotment of bishops. Canterbury therefore kept the position of supreme authority it attained under Theodore, who found only two bishops in office, one of whom he removed. By the time of his death England had been divided into 15 dioceses – four in the north, four in the midlands, two in East Anglia, and five in the south. Two more bishoprics added soon afterwards make a total of seventeen, lying within the frontiers of the future kingdom of England, half of which have continued down to the present day: namely Canterbury, London, Rochester, Winchester, Worcester, Hereford, Lichfield, and York.

While the dioceses provided the framework of the new Church organization, its heart was in the monasteries. Both Augustine and Theodore were monks, who viewed with sympathy the spread of monastic houses whose inmates, unlike the wandering Celtic monks already described, lived a strictly disciplined religious life within the walls. The Rule devised in Italy by St Benedict, which required the monk to divide the day between hours of worship and hours of work and to perform every duty in strict obedience to his abbot or other superior, found increasing favour. Such Benedictine monasteries were richly endowed by kings and thegns, some of whom eventually retired from the world to end their days as monks. The monastic buildings, and especially the great church round which all other activities were centred, were more elaborate than any structures seen in England since the days of the Romans, expert stone-masons and glassworkers being brought over from the continent for their embellishment. Most of the cathedral cities held an important monastery, such as that which contained the school at Canterbury. Malmesbury became a great centre of scholarship in the west, and Peterborough is believed to have evangelized the fenland; but for special reasons this early monasticism flowered chiefly in the north.

Golden Age of Northumbria

The conflict of ideas which had culminated in the synod of Whitby gave a stimulus to the whole life of the northern Church. The Celtic tradition there had still to produce its greatest saint in

Cuthbert, a shepherd boy from the Lammermuirs with a well-attested gift of second sight. He trudged the hills as a solitary missionary, from whom 'no man dared to hide the secrets of his heart'; then spent eight years in lonely contemplation on Farne Island, emerging with reluctance to serve as prior and bishop and returning to die there, almost starving, with birds and beasts as his companions, a humble and heroic figure of legendary sanctity. But it was the new link with Rome which made possible the great cultural achievements for which the old Northumbria is still remembered, so many centuries after its brief period of leadership.

The beautifully carved stone crosses, unrivalled in the Europe of that day, have already been mentioned. Another outlet for religious zeal in alliance with artistic skill was provided by the task of embellishing new copies of the scriptures, so as to rival or excel the fine specimens of copyists' work brought back by pilgrims and others from the continent. Only a few years after Cuthbert's death in 687, his monastery of Lindisfarne produced a gospel book for use at the altar, whose decorations brilliantly combine the Celtic love of nature and imaginative ornament with traditional religious themes derived from Italian manuscripts. It has even been suggested that the maze-like patterns bordering the sacred text are in themselves a form of worship, an expression of reverence for life's mysteries. At all events, the richness of the achievement lifts us far above the squabbles of half-forgotten kingdoms to gain a new respect for some of the aims cherished in a distant past.

> As we look at these pages [writes a leading modern historian] we think of Eadfrith the monk working away in a hut, dark, draughty, exposed to the storms of wind and rain that sweep up from the North Sea. He works month after month, year after year, completing his one masterpiece, writing his bold half-uncial script, interlacing his birds and hounds with unfailing accuracy and infinite patience, to the glory of God; illuminating his folios with colours that cannot be adequately reproduced by any mechanical process, colours which glow like the stained glass of medieval church windows.[1]

Fifty miles south of Lindisfarne the new monastery of Jarrow,

[1] R. H. Hodgkin: *A History of the Anglo-Saxons*, Vol. I. p. 360.

created directly in the Roman tradition, provided the setting for virtually the whole life of Bede, the 'father of English history'. Our general knowledge of the events from the landing of Augustine to the completion of the *Ecclesiastical History of the English Nation* in A.D. 731 rests securely on Bede's work. For, although the *History* was only one among his thirty-six works, all of which had the edification of the reader as their central aim, Bede was something more than a painstaking and judicious writer compiling a narrative in scholarly medieval Latin: he had the true historian's faculty for composing a single whole out of many disconnected fragments of information. His completion of an English version of St John's gospel as he lay dying on the floor of his cell is a vivid reminder of the immense industriousness which Bede must have brought to all his tasks. It also underlines the fact that at this period the English began to write in their own language.

Orally transmitted songs and lays accompanied and perhaps celebrated the Anglo-Saxon invasion; the Sutton Hoo treasure includes a harp. Caedmon's 'Hymn to the Creator', the work of a herdsman in the Northumbrian monastery at Whitby, begins a second period, in which religious poetry no doubt predominated. But, apart from Bede's transmission of Caedmon's lines, all that is left is the striking 'Dream of the Rood' – the Crucifixion as seen by the Cross itself – carved in ancient runic letters on the Ruthwell cross. No early prose literature survives at all. However, it is reasonable to place within one or two generations after Bede the unknown author of the great narrative poem of *Beowulf*. Although the scene is laid in heathen Scandinavia and the powers of evil with which Beowulf contends belong to the world of dragons and haunted meres, the poet appears to write from a Christian background. In any case, the qualities he most extols, such as courage, loyalty, and the spirit of adventure, were qualities of which the Church made abundant use.

We see this in the group of eighth-century Englishmen who contributed to the progress of Christianity in what were then remoter parts of western Europe. Less than a hundred years after the landing of Augustine, a Northumbrian monk named Willibrord was given the authority of an archbishop when he went out across the North Sea as a missionary to the Frisians. He established his see at Utrecht, where he added a new province to the Church, and ventured as far afield as Denmark. Still more remarkable was the work of a West Saxon, Boniface, who was the main instrument of the papacy in the conversion of Germany and who was eventually martyred on a further mission to the Frisians. 'Probably the most able missionary ever produced by a north European country,' says a recent Church history.[1] Both these leaders had numerous English men and some English women as their helpers. A kinsman and biographer of Willibrord was the scholar Alcuin, master of the monastic school at York, who in the last decades of the century carried the best of Northumbrian culture to the court of Charlemagne at Aachen, where he acted as head of the palace school and general religious adviser to the all-powerful ruler of the Franks and founder of the Holy Roman Empire. Thus the cultural influence of England upon the continent stood higher than in any other period before the eighteenth century.

Church and State

Nevertheless, the correspondence of Bede, Alcuin, and other Church leaders suggests that these achievements in the mission field were accompanied by some falling-off in religious zeal at home, particularly in the monasteries. But the truth may be that the story of the conversion highlights the triumphs of the faith and passes gently over failures, to which a more critical age drew attention. It is much easier to trace the growth of Christian institutions than Christian conduct, but we may venture to consider briefly by what means the latter was shaped.

The Church disciplined its children partly through the development of law, on which the clergy had great influence. Marriage and divorce were more strictly regulated than before, and civil penalties were used against ecclesiastical offences, such as delaying baptism, neglecting fast-days, or working on Sunday. It was the policy of the Church to get the number of capital offences reduced, since they left no room for repentance, but to insist on the sanctity of the oath, so that it probably became harder to escape trial by the old method of accumulating weighty persons to swear to one's

[1] J. Godfrey: *The Church in Anglo-Saxon England*, p. 230.

innocence. Instead, the clergy themselves took part in trials by ordeal: for the water that rejected the guilty party by causing him to float, the hot iron or boiling water that made his hand fester, and the morsel that choked him were all regarded as infallible instruments of a divine justice. As for the countless minor infringements of the Church's teaching of the ten commandments and the seven deadly sins (as enumerated by Pope Gregory), some result was achieved through an annual confession, preceding the Christmas festival and accompanied by such penalties as a bread-and-water diet. But in most of the slowly forming parishes of rural England the struggle to win a living from the soil, with the ever-present fear of starvation as a sequel to famine or war, must have made the repression of heathen superstitions and the cultivation of newer and milder virtues a very slow business.

The institutions of the state, however, were quickly modified. Written laws began with the conversion: in the time of Augustine those of Kent already prescribed twelvefold compensation for any theft of Church property. The Church also introduced parchment charters, known as 'land-books', so that land given to the Church could be exempted from customary obligations, including the right of the direct heir to reclaim it after the donor's death. Since the payment of church dues and, later, tithe were compulsory, these voluntary gifts of land went chiefly to the creation of monastic and episcopal estates, often of great size, which would be the first to benefit by the introduction of new crops and agricultural techniques from the continent. In return for all this, the Church gave the state new possibilities of development. For the first time, kings had councillors whose knowledge extended to the world outside England; skilled draftsmen, who could write in Latin, the international language; and clerks to keep all kinds of records and accounts.

Rise and Decline of Mercia

Since the bishops were appointed by the kings, the fortunes of the Church were to some extent tied up with the wearisome conflicts between the kingdoms. The political strength of Northumbria began to decline about the time of the synod of Whitby. In the north her attempted advance beyond the Forth was decisively defeated by the Picts at Nechtansmere in 685, and in the following century the marshes west of the Humber marked the southern limit of Northumbrian influence. The leadership passed eventually to Mercia, the midland kingdom, which extended its direct rule to East Anglia and the south-east and had the overlordship of Wessex. Though Mercia never developed a proper capital, for a few years a third archbishopric was established at Lichfield by the pope, who recognized Offa of Mercia as 'king of the English'. The growth of commerce in his reign was marked by the introduction of a standard silver penny, which was the main Anglo-Saxon coin for the next three centuries; but of Offa as a person virtually nothing is known, except the significant fact that he was able to negotiate on almost equal terms with Charlemagne.

His name survives on the map, however, as the creator of Offa's Dyke, the most important frontier line that has been built in Britain since the Roman Walls. It connects the Wye and the Dee approximately along the course of the modern frontier of Wales-and-Monmouthshire. Mound and ditch together still retain in some places a height of 30 feet, but the most interesting feature is the engineering skill shown in the choice of a route which almost everywhere commands the approach from the west – except for the most densely forested areas, where no dyke was needed. But the dyke was more of an agreed boundary than a fortification, and the evidence of place-names shows that some English villages were sacrificed to obtain Welsh agreement. Farther north, Offa's peace with the Welsh had its counterpart in the unchronicled withdrawal of Celtic power beyond the modern Scottish boundary, so that for a time there was even an English diocese based on Whithorn in Galloway.

Only in the south-west was the making of England to proceed one step farther before its temporary unmaking at the hands of the Vikings. This was the work of Wessex, the last leader in the unification of the English kingdoms.

In the seventh century the West Saxons took Exeter and, according to their chronicle, 'drove the Britons as far as the sea', which is perhaps a bombastic way of saying 'beyond the Tamar'. But their strength then became exhausted in unsuccessful encounters with the Mercians. West of Bath the earthwork of the Wansdyke perhaps marked the boundary between the two kingdoms; farther east, even the upper Thames Valley was lost by Wessex for a time. But after the death of Offa in 796 its fortunes revived, and the ninth century opened with an initial subjugation of the Cornishmen. Then, after making themselves masters of the south-east as well as the extreme south-west, the West Saxons in 825 succeeded in defeating the Mercians in battle and achieved at least a shadowy supremacy over the whole of England. Thirteen years later, the suppression of a final rebellion in Cornwall marks a more definite stage in English history: there was no longer any Celtic kingdom in England. But a new stage had already begun, for what had given the Cornish strength to rebel was an alliance with 'a great ship-army' of Vikings.

5

THE IMPACT OF SCANDINAVIA

In the year 793 there occurred off the north-east coast of Britain a grim portent of horrors to come. The peaceful monastery of Lindisfarne was suddenly attacked by raiders from across the North Sea, who robbed it of its riches and massacred some of the monks. The Vikings had come, and the whole Christian world of the north was appalled at their coming. 'Never have terrors like these appeared in Britain,' wrote Alcuin of York; 'it was not thought possible that such havoc could be made.' But such disasters were now to be common enough: in 794 Bede's monastery at Jarrow was attacked, and next it was the turn of Iona. If the astonishment that such things could happen disappeared, the horror remained.

The homelands of these pirates were the Scandinavian peninsula and Denmark – the lands of the Norwegians, Swedes and Danes. As far as Britain is concerned, however, the people on the east side of the peninsula can be ignored, for Swedish expansion was predominantly eastwards.

Viking Voyages and Ships

The Norwegians were the first to take to the seas, and for them the motive was mainly survival. Their population was small – perhaps no more than 200,000 – but the land they occupied was harsh, and wresting a living from it was a daily struggle: the attraction of softer lands to the west, which they became increasingly aware of, was too great to resist. It was as settlers in empty lands and as traders that they first set out, but when news was brought back of easily won riches in the west, enterprises of war became the most attractive to them, and it is as warriors that they are most vividly remembered.

The bulk of Norwegian expansion was directly to the west,

rather than down the North Sea to the south, and the men in their questing ships headed first to the Shetlands, then south to the Orkneys and Hebrides, following the west coast of Scotland till they came to Ireland. Here they divided: some passed down the west coast and some down the east, from which they also reached the Isle of Man. Ireland, rather than Norway itself, was later to be the main base for Norwegian attacks on Britain. The Norwegians also made much longer voyages, sailing via the Faeroes to Iceland and Greenland, and eventually to North America.

The Danes, who were much more numerous than the Norwegians, were compelled by their geographical position to take a closer interest in the affairs of Europe. At the end of the eighth and the beginning of the ninth century, the dominating force in western Europe was the expanding empire of Charlemagne, the king of the Franks. This empire, through its recent conquest of the Frisians and the continental Saxons, had expanded as far as the southern boundary of Denmark. For the Danes this was both a threat and an opportunity – a threat that they might be absorbed next, and an opportunity for their own expansion southwards. Earlier, their expansion by sea in this direction had been blocked by the powerful Frisian fleet; now Charlemagne had broken this fleet and the way to the south lay open. About the middle of the ninth century the Danes took full advantage of this opportunity, being greatly helped by the weakness of the empire of Charlemagne in the years after his death. The long-ships of the Danes sought out the weak places of the Christian world and, as the booty of ransacked monasteries came home to Denmark, the passion for plunder and destruction gripped the people.

For the Danes the route of adventure lay west and south-west to eastern England and south to the Channel and the rich lands on both sides of it. Beyond this, they mingled with the Norwegians and often fought against them.

When Alcuin of York wrote of the sacking of Lindisfarne, he said of the Vikings that 'it was not thought possible that they could have made the journey'. Yet Alcuin's ancestors had made a similar, if shorter, journey and under more primitive conditions. At least the Viking ships had sails, so that their crews were not condemned to row them the rough journey to Britain.

We need not be so astonished as was Alcuin at the distance these Viking long-ships could travel. After one of them had been excavated from a burial mound at Gokstad in Norway, a full-scale modern replica was sailed across the Atlantic in four weeks. The ships were of a similar size to the Saxon ships of Nydam and Sutton Hoo, but had four main differences; a mast slightly forward of amidships to take a single square sail, rowlocks cut in the hull (with shutters for use when the oars were not needed), a tiller to work the steerboard, and an external keel for greater stability. They had two parallel ridge-poles running the length of the ship, across which an awning could be spread so that, when the ships were in harbour, their crews could sleep in them as though in tents. At sea, the crews slept in skin bags between the rowing benches. The vessels were clinker-built and in these early days probably had no more than twenty oars a side. Later on, bigger ships were used, including a type of broad-beamed trading vessel more suitable for settlers with their families and gear.

'Ships came from the east, ready for war,' said a Norwegian poet of the time, 'with grinning heads and carven beaks, impelled with desire for battle.' And the Viking long-ships, sailing towards the coastline of England, must truly have been an awe-inspiring sight. Their carved dragon prows plunging through the water, their billowing sails striped in red, blue or green, and the colourful round shields of the crews suspended over the sides of the ships, gave out so full an air of confidence that men had to be brave indeed not to feel their knees weaken at the sight. Nor would the gleaming Viking weapons lessen the terror the ships inspired – spears, swords, great two-handed battle-axes, and short bows, even the last being deadly enough when the enemy was beyond the range of the swinging axes.

Establishment of the Danelaw

All western Europe was for a time the playground of the Viking battle-axes, and the duchy of Normandy, carved out of north-west France, was only the most lasting of many mainland annexations. So far as England is concerned, the last third of the ninth century was the period when unplanned raids gave place to planned conquest. This phase, which was interrupted by a long period of English recovery, was completed early in the eleventh century, when Cnut the Dane ruled all England. The Vikings who came to this country were predominantly Danish, as is clear from the name Danelaw, which was given to the large, mainly eastern, region where Danish law and land tenure became established before the close of the ninth century. Its northern limit was the Tees valley, and in the south the estuary of the Thames. On the west it included the Lancashire coast, south of which the general line of demarcation was the Watling Street. Within this area a smaller district of Norwegian settlement was established rather later by a migration from Ireland to the north-west coast, stretching from the Wirral peninsula to Cumberland, and even carrying some Norwegians across the Pennines to set up a short-lived Norse 'Kingdom of York'.

Alfred and the Unification of England

The Scandinavian settlers, whether Danes or Norwegians, were never driven out of the half of England they had made their own. How their numbers compared with those of the English who survived the wars of conquest we do not know; but even if they were generally no more than a minority, they were clearly a dominant minority who set their stamp upon the whole life of the Danelaw region. It was fortunate for the English that their conversion was quickly accomplished – the archbishop was able to return to York as early as 878 – and that the languages of the two peoples were no great barrier. Even so, it is realistic to picture several generations of English wives living in considerable dread of their Viking husbands and many generations of Englishmen deploring the loss of the best land to men with whom they dare not quarrel.

Enough has been said to show the enormous general impact of the Viking conquests upon England. But it would have been still greater, had not a period of English recovery (referred to above) been interposed by the work of Alfred, king of Wessex from 871 to 899 and one of the most striking personalities in the history of England. When the other English kingdoms had succumbed, Wessex, which had only recently begun to play the leading part, turned back the tide of battle sufficiently to achieve a division of territory between Saxon and Dane. It is possible to point to some advantages in the Wessex position – that it had expanded to include the key area of the south-east, adjoining the continent; that it had better-defined natural frontiers than Mercia or Northumbria; and – most interesting – that its laws suggest a greater success in amalgamating Celtic remnants into a Saxon community. Be this as it may, the imprint of Alfred's own personality can be seen in the whole of the strategy by which the English were rescued from a truly desperate position. It had three main elements which gained him success: the building of forts, the organization of an army and the creation of a fleet.

Alfred saw that much of the power of the Danish armies lay in their fortified camps. From these they could sally out when it was safe, and to them return when things became difficult. In the midlands they based their power upon great permanent fortifications – the 'five boroughs' of Stamford, Leicester, Derby, Nottingham and Lincoln. Alfred determined to imitate them. Round the borders of Wessex, and in the interior too, the fortifications went up: at such places as Hastings, Chichester, Southampton, Exeter and Oxford. By the end of Alfred's life, there was no village in Wessex more than twenty miles from a fortified place. Each of these 'burhs' was the centre of a military district and was responsible for its defence, and the inhabitants of each had a duty to man the fortress and to fight in the district round it when necessary.

The nucleus of Alfred's army was provided by the king's thegns, who were the great nobles about the court, and by his personal bodyguard of retainers. But in time of war there was also the 'fyrd', the force of the shire under the ealdorman and many lesser thegns. Since its members were mostly farmers, it was difficult to keep a force of men constantly together, when farm work had also to be carried on. Alfred therefore divided the fyrd into two parts, so that men could alternate fighting with farming.

Alfred was almost the only ruler of the time who saw that if the Vikings, who were supreme by sea, were to be defeated, then it must at least partly be by fighting them in their own element. In his last years he obtained Frisian help in designing his own ships, which had as many as thirty oars a side, so that bigger vessels had to be built in the Scandinavian lands to keep up with him. The fleet he had created was soon numbered in hundreds, and was strong enough to defend the shores of England for a century. The recorded beginnings of the navy are therefore to be found in the reign of Alfred.

By such measures as these, Wessex became the heart of the resistance to the Danes and the most important of the English kingdoms. But the power of the Wessex monarchy is shown in more than the mere holding of the Danish attacks – it is revealed in the eventual recognition of its supremacy by the greater part of Britain.

The result of Alfred's military efforts was a treaty with the Danes, which marked out the limits between his territory and theirs. The English frontier at that time ran from the Thames up to Bedford; from there along the Ouse to Watling Street and so to the Welsh border. Thus Alfred controlled as a sub-kingdom the part of Mercia which had not been swallowed up by the Danelaw. His son, Edward the Elder, advanced the power of Wessex to the Humber. In the time of Edward's son, Athelstan, the Scandinavian kingdom of York was conquered and reunited with the English lands beyond, so that Alfred's great-grandson Edgar, crowned near the end of his reign in 973 at Bath, was king of a united England. Since Edgar's overlordship was in some sense recognized by the other kings of the island, and since his reign was an interval of peace, prosperity, and monastic revival preceding the second wave of Danish invasion and conquest, this will be a convenient point at which to notice what effect the Vikings had had on the fortunes of Scotland and Wales.

The Viking Impact on Scotland and Wales

The thinly populated Scottish Highlands, with the clusters of islands along the natural Norwegian route to the west, had more to offer to settlers than to plunderers. Accordingly, in the ninth century the Shetlands, Orkneys, Hebrides, and the mainland as far south as the Beauly Firth passed under Norwegian sovereignty, which was not seriously challenged for the next three hundred years. Other attacks were directed against the Picts from Ireland,

and it seems reasonable to suppose that the weakening effect of the Viking impact upon the Pictish kingdom partly explains its acceptance of a union with its smaller neighbour, Scottish Dalriada. At all events, the accession of Kenneth MacAlpin in 843, though followed by some Pictish resistance to the rule of a Scottish king, created a lasting monarchy which served (like the Wessex dynasty in England) as the basis of opposition to Viking conquest.

The details of the process by which southern Scotland became added to the new monarchy created in the north are not wholly clear. Cumbria apparently was overrun by the English and subsequently handed over to the king of Scots, as a safeguard against attack from Ireland, in the days of the Scandinavian kingdom of York. Strathclyde became Scottish through a further union of crowns early in the eleventh century, so for a time the western flank of the united Scottish kingdom stretched down to Cumberland and northern Westmorland. On the east coast, however, something like the modern border was established in the reign of Edgar, when Lothian was granted to the kings of Scots, a holding which was much later confirmed by Scottish success in battle.

Although Wales was exposed to attack from the Viking kingdoms in Ireland and the Isle of Man and was also accessible from the south along the Bristol Channel, its resistance was for a long time remarkably successful. Even the exposed island of Anglesey was protected by the strong rulers of the northern kingdom of Gwynedd, and in the first half of the tenth century conditions were sufficiently settled for a revised code of law to have been issued to some kind of representative gathering by a ruler called Howell the Good, who claimed to be king of all the Welsh. His death in 950 was followed by a period of widespread devastation by the Vikings, but place-names show that their settlements were very largely confined to the exposed south coast, where they developed such ports as Swansea and Tenby.

Institutions of the Wessex Monarchy

Of the three countries in the island England alone was fated to suffer a complete Viking conquest. But before we pass on to the decline and fall of the Wessex monarchy under Edgar's son, Ethelred the Redeless, the West Saxon institutions of government deserve our attention. Their influence survived, and is part of the English heritage. This is strikingly illustrated by the continuity of the coronation service, still in the twentieth century conducted in part according to the ritual used in the reign of Edgar. In those days the throne was not hereditary, but was passed on in accordance with the choice of the previous king and the agreement of the 'moot' or council of wise men (*witan*), so that the solemn religious coronation of the sovereign was an important practical ratification of his authority: hence the points of resemblance between the modern coronation ceremony and the ordination of a priest.

The king did not rule from one centre or hold his council meetings in one place. Instead, he made his presence felt by travelling about the country accompanied by some of his leading advisers and by his clerks, who represent the beginnings of a civil service. Yet, even though the power of Wessex came to extend over the whole of England, the king did not hold court very frequently outside Wessex and his treasury became more or less fixed at Winchester. London was not the natural administrative centre of England at this time, because it lay too close to Danish territory – indeed, Alfred had to wrest it from the possession of the Danes – and was in any case traditionally part of old Mercia rather than of Wessex.

The power of every king depended largely on the ease with which he could collect revenue. The revenue of the late Saxon kings depended on two main sources: the money, or often the food, that came from the royal estates, and the profits from fines in the royal courts. Modern forms of taxation began with the 'danegeld', which was first levied on a national basis in 991. Long after it had ceased to be required for buying off the Danes, the name continued in use for a tax on every 'hide'[1] of land, which was raised for military and other purposes.

One of the royal powers from the earliest times was the issue of coins and, from the tenth century, only the kings of Wessex were able to exercise this right in England, though the coinage of

[1] See p. 64

Wessex was considerably older than this. The dies for the coins came to be cut only in London, and these were then distributed to the numerous towns which were authorized to operate a mint. For many centuries the only coin struck was the silver penny, though other denominations existed on paper – for the keeping of accounts – such as the pound, the mark (which was two-thirds of a pound) and the shilling. Every coin bore on one side the head of the king and on the other the name of the place where it was minted. English coinage had such a high reputation in Europe that English minters were brought into Scandinavia to supervise the issue there of a coinage closely modelled upon that of Wessex. The Wessex kings also had a form of receipt, when money for taxes was paid into the treasury at Winchester, in the shape of a 'tally'. This was a stick, usually of hazel-wood, which could be marked across with notches of various lengths to represent a sum of money: it was then split lengthwise, so that the notches showed in each piece. If any doubt arose later, the amount could be proved by laying the pieces together.

No king of Wessex could rule England directly from the centre, even with the help of the magnates who composed the Witan. In the delegation of his power he was helped by the larger and smaller divisions into which England had by the tenth century been organized. The largest division was the county, or shire, and its most important royal official the ealdorman, replaced eventually by the Danish 'earl'. In the time of the Danish invasions there was some danger that the powers of the earls might rival those of the king, all the more so since some earls ruled over more than a single county. Another important official was the shire-reeve or sheriff, who had both legal and taxing functions. The shires were divided into 'hundreds'. The size of these varied considerably and their origin is unknown, but in the west Midlands at least they often represented a hundred hides; a hide was the smallest division of land in Saxon England, traditionally the amount that would support a single family.

All these divisions were useful in the collection of taxes, and they were also important in the administration of justice. Besides the king's court, moving as he himself moved, there were shire courts and the hundred courts. In all these royal officials presided, accompanied in the shire court by the bishop. But there was also a part to be played by ordinary peasants, who were expected to be able to answer questions of fact, such as who were the holders of particular pieces of land.

Since land was the kind of property which mattered most, the activities of royal officials are known to us chiefly through carefully preserved documents concerning land ownership. In the earliest days grants of land must have been made verbally, but as soon as there were clerics available to act as clerks (the words are originally the same) the recipients would wish to have solid documentary evidence of possession. Before the Norman conquest such evidence was mainly provided by 'land-books': charters written in Latin and often in the most high-flown style. A sentence from one of Athelstan's charters runs as follows:

If . . . anyone puffed up with the pride of arrogance shall try to destroy . . . this little document . . . let him know that on the last and fearful day of assembly, when the trumpet of the archangel is clanging the call and bodies are leaving the foul graveyards, he will burn with Judas . . . in eternal confusion, in the devouring flames of blazing torments, in punishment without end.

But such lofty proclamations slowly gave way to more prosaic 'writs'. These were notifications in English, sealed with the royal seal, which became the normal method by which the king communicated his will on any matter to his officials throughout the country.

Revival of Learning and the Church

All these things – success in war, in the unification of England, and in the development of a strong system of government – raised the prestige of the monarchy of Wessex. But there was another factor – the encouragement given by the kings of Wessex to learning, which in quite a different way made Wessex the centre of England.

It was Alfred who, in the time of the first Danish invasions, attempted to halt the decay of learning in Wessex. 'I cannot find anything better in man than that he should know,' he said, 'and nothing worse than that he should be ignorant.' Therefore he gathered round him a group of scholars, founded a palace school for the education of the nobility, demanded that his officials should try to educate themselves, and translated Latin books into English. In these translations he thought of himself as a woodcutter in the forest of knowledge: 'I neither came home with a single load, nor did it suit me to bring home all the wood, even if I could have carried it. In each tree I saw something that I required at home.' In such a way also, Alfred gathered from the legal codes of earlier Saxon kings material for his new code of laws and, as well as cutting what had been planted by other men, he planted a rich seed of his own in the starting of the Anglo-Saxon Chronicle.

Yet the monasteries, the natural allies of the king in the revival of learning, could not help him: they were the worst sufferers from the raids of the Danes. By the time of Alfred the monastic life had broken down completely: there was hardly a single community that continued its measured routine and few monastic buildings remained in use. And there was the same disorganization in the Church as a whole. Over large parts of England the bishops ceased to function and in many parishes public worship had entirely died out: it seems likely that between 850 and 900 no new churches were built at all.

This problem, of course, was international, for all western Europe had suffered from the Viking raids; accordingly, the revival of church and monastic life came at almost the same time in many countries. This revival started in France, in the monastery of Cluny in the first half of the tenth century. In England it came about rather later, when continental reforms were introduced by Dunstan, an abbot of Glastonbury whom Edgar made archbishop of Canterbury. Old monasteries were revived and some new ones created, all based on a strict observance of the Benedictine Rule. In 1066 the number of monks and nuns was only about a thousand, but their influence on church life was such that by that date every diocese had at least once had a monk as its bishop.

With the revival of the monasteries, Alfred's earlier efforts to encourage learning could not be taken further. Two leading figures at the end of the tenth century were Aelfric and Wulfstan, the one head of a monastic school and the other archbishop of York. By their translations of Latin books into Old English and by their own writings, they gave the language a firm grammatical basis and prose style. A long step was taken towards the education of the ordinary parish priest, making it possible for him to understand the Latin in which his services were held and in which the Bible was available. With the writing of books came an advance in the art of producing them, so that English illuminated manuscripts became for a time the finest in Europe, and Latin books, copied in England, were in wide demand on the Continent.

Loss of Freedom by the Peasant

But the achievements of the Wessex monarchy would not have been possible without the work of the peasants (ceorls or 'churls') who tilled the soil. It is therefore important to notice a slow change in their position and the reasons for it. Even before the Danish invasions many landholders in Wessex were in some way dependent upon lords. Some of these lords or thegns were men close to the king, who owned very large and scattered estates, but most were lesser thegns, with anything over five hides of land, or such merchants as had crossed the sea three times in their own ships. Since each hide represented in principle the amount of land traditionally allocated in that part of the country to a single peasant farm, a thegn with five hides may be presumed to have had at least four 'churls' as tenants. Before long, during the Danish invasions, these 'churls' not only paid rent but worked for a part of each week on the land of their lord. In fine, throughout much of England the peasant lost status, by the deterioration of his farm while he was on service with the fyrd; by Danish devastations, which might make him dependent on a lord for the buildings, stock and tools needed for a new start; and by debts incurred to pay the danegeld.

Danish Conquest Completed

In the reign of Ethelred, younger son of Edgar, payment of increasingly heavy sums of danegeld failed to buy off the invaders.

In 1002, 24,000 lb of silver were paid, in 1006 36,000 lb, and in 1012 42,000 lb, causing the whole kingdom to groan under the hopeless strain and leaving posterity to wonder that the system of collection did not break down. By 1016 a Danish king's son, Cnut, was master of all England, at the end of a struggle in which Ethelred abundantly illustrated his lack of counsel or 'rede'.

As in the earlier wars of the Wessex monarchy, there were episodes of great heroism, but they no longer took place within the framework of a master-plan. We must be content to recall the poet's picture of the scene at Maldon in the bird-haunted Essex marshes, where the Saxon ealdorman was killed opposing a Danish landing and his followers' choice was to die with him rather than to seek safety in flight.

> *Here lies our lord, all hewn down–*
> *A hero in the dust; ever may mourn now*
> *He who thinks to turn from this battle-play.*
> *I am old in years: I will not turn hence.*
> *But I by the side of my lord,*
> *By so dear a man, think to lie.*

Nevertheless, it is important to realize that Cnut, a Christian since childhood and eventually king of Denmark and Norway as well as England, was a highly successful ruler, whose seventeen-year reign brought England within the orbit of a North Sea maritime empire. If he had not died at forty, this link might well have had a lasting effect on English fortunes. As it was, a reign in which some Scandinavian landowners became established in every county of England is chiefly memorable as marking the climax of Scandinavian influences that had been important at least since the time of Alfred. What, then, was the Scandinavian contribution to the making of England?

Its Lasting Effects

In the first place, the Danes of the Danelaw and the Norwegians of the north-west – like the Norwegians of the Scottish islands – were sufficiently numerous to alter the make-up of the local

population, a fact which the modern map confirms. In Lincolnshire, for instance, the names of 212 settlements have the Scandinavian termination -by; together with -thorpe, which indicates a
rather larger type of settlement, it is common throughout a broad
belt of territory between – but excluding – the counties of Durham
and Northampton. In the north-west, again, a high proportion
of words used to describe natural features are Scandinavian, as in
the case of fell, force (for waterfall), beck, and tarn, together with
such settlement terms as garth (for enclosure) and thwaite (for
clearing). The Normans at the time of the Domesday Book inquiry
found a much higher proportion of freemen in the former Danelaw than in other regions of England. Perhaps it is not fanciful
to suppose that the infusion of Scandinavian stock gave the north
of England a sterner and more forthright character, which is still
sometimes held to distinguish its sons and daughters from those
of the slower and kindlier south.

We are on surer ground in pointing to the increase of trade,
which even Scandinavian pirates practised as an avocation. Anglo-
Saxon coins are to be found in ninth-century Norwegian graves,
and although the great hoards of coins which occur later on in such
commercial centres as the Baltic island of Gotland contain a
noticeably high proportion from the reign of Ethelred, there is no
doubt that trade as well as tribute flowed eastwards across the
North Sea. The stimulus given to east coast ports, together with
the Danish cultivation of new land in Lincolnshire and parts of
Norfolk, established the position of the eastern counties as the
most prosperous region of medieval England. On the west coast,
too, there was a lively trade between Chester and Bristol and
Scandinavian Ireland, particularly it seems in slaves. All this came
to a head in the reign of Cnut, who gave Danish merchants privileges of a year's residence in London and unrestricted travel to
markets and fairs throughout the realm; he also obtained concessions from foreign rulers, enabling his subjects, pilgrims and
traders alike, to follow the route up the Rhine and over the Alps
to Rome.

Overseas commerce, seamanship, and the art of shipbuilding
must all have derived some lasting benefit, but the most obvious
long-term result was the growth of town life. Alfred, as we have

seen, copied from the Scandinavian invaders his practice of creating towns as military centres, where a population of traders and others tended naturally to congregate within the shelter of earthen or stone defences. Apart from the Five Boroughs of the east midlands, York and Norwich may be instanced as major provincial cities where the Scandinavian element was particularly strong. But London, which employed more than twice as many minters to strike its money as the West Saxon capital of Winchester, was clearly the most important of English towns. And there the new influence can be traced, not only in such church dedications as St Clement Danes and St Olave's, Southwark, but even in a complete network of petty divisional courts called by the Scandinavian name of *husting*.

Law, too, was one of their words and special interests, having a considerable bearing on trade. Both 'by-law' and 'outlaw' refer back to Scandinavian legal practices, enforced in courts of the *wapentakes*, which in six eastern counties permanently replaced the Saxon hundreds; the very name of 'Danelaw' is a reminder that the reconquest by Alfred and his successors did not affect legal institutions. Particular interest attaches to the practice by which in each district of the Danelaw twelve thegns were required to present for trial such persons as were known by common report to be wrongdoers: here we have one of the origins of the modern jury. Thus a period which begins with havoc and continues with hardly less barbarous wars of conquest can also be seen in retrospect to have made a considerable positive contribution to the growth of the British people.

6

THE FRANCO–NORMAN CONQUEST

CNUT's North Sea empire of England, Denmark, and Norway was held together by long seaborne communications which would in any case have endangered its permanence: even the great prestige of Cnut could not roll back the waves so that the North Sea vanished. But the immediate cause of the breakdown of his empire was not so much the geographical factors as a lack of heirs. Because he and his two sons died young, within twenty-six years of Cnut's accession the direct line of his descendants had come to an end. But, if the throne of Denmark could supply no natural successor, that of Alfred's house, could in the person of Ethelred's son, Edward, known for his piety as 'the Confessor'. So the old Saxon line was restored and, if Edward had had sons to follow him, 1066 would not have been the year of England's greatest revolution. But when he died childless on January 5th, 1066, the question of who should rule England was again thrown open.

For military reasons Harold, the ambitious earl of Wessex, was accepted in preference to a youthful great-nephew of Edward. At Stamfordbridge in September he justified himself by winning a great victory over his namesake, the king of Norway, a dangerous rival claimant to whom York had already submitted. Less than three weeks later, under the handicap of a forced march he faced a second rival at Hastings, where the better disciplined army of the Norman leader won the day-long battle. The death of Harold on the stricken field; the coronation of William the Conqueror at Westminster on Christmas Day; and his punitive expeditions, which reached a climax in 1069, when the long-remembered 'harrying of the north' stamped out the last embers of resistance in the Danelaw – these were the remaining events with which the contest for the English throne was brought decisively to an end.

The Norman–French conquerors are vividly portrayed in the 231-foot-long Bayeux tapestry, woven before the end of the century and subject therefore to the possible scrutiny of some of those concerned. It shows the ships they came in, and the horses and gear which accompanied these seasoned campaigners. It shows the rough-and-ready castles they built to safeguard their bases at Pevensey and Hastings. It shows the chainmail armour, conical helmets, kite-shaped shields, and long lances used in the great battle. Above all, its 72 scenes, both before and during the decisive battle, illustrate the superior discipline and organizing capacity which these descendants of the Vikings had developed in their lands in France. These qualities were now to permeate the life of England and, a little later, that of Scotland and Wales, together with a distinctive Norman culture, of which the Confessor had indeed given his subjects a slight foretaste – in the architecture of his abbey at Westminster, for instance, and in his preferment of Norman clerics to English bishoprics.

Plate 11. *Stem-post of a Viking Ship.* Probably 8th century: found in the River Scheldt, Belgium, it is 57 inches long. (Cf. text p. 58.)

Plate 12. *Remains of the Saxon burh at Wallingford, Berkshire.* The earliest defences of Wallingford date from about the time of Alfred and were 3,300 yards in circuit, of which 3,030 (including the river front) can still be traced. The best preserved parts (which this picture illustrates) are on the west, where the earthwork stands ten or twelve feet above the inner floor – and still more above the bottom of the outside ditch. (Cf. text p. 60.)

Plate 13. *The Saxon stand at Hastings (Bayeux Tapestry).* This shows the English, on foot, presenting their 'shield wall' to the mounted Norman invaders. Armour on both sides is almost identical – though, where round shields are shown in the tapestry, they are always English, for they were not suited to mounted men. Weapons show differences, in that some English have the Danish axe and appear to rely more on spears than the Normans – perhaps because they were short of archers. The tailed banners on both sides are 'gonfanons' – a mark of authority. (Cf. text p. 72.)

Plate 14. *Motte and Bailey castle at Pleshey, Essex.* An excellent example of a simple, early post-Conquest, motte and bailey, with its high mound rising fifty feet above its moat and dominating the bailey on the nearer side of the existing bridge. Both motte and bailey would have been topped by a timber palisade, and there is evidence from a 1922 excavation that a later stone building was erected on the motte – perhaps in the 14th century. There may have been a second bailey on the far side of the motte, within the limits of the semi-circular road shown in this picture. (Cf. text pp. 82–3.)

Plate 11

Plate 12

Plate 13

Plate 14

Landholders and Their Military Obligations

The greatest change of all, perhaps, was the introduction of a new system of English land-holding. It is said that, when duke William landed at Pevensey, he slipped and fell on the wet sand, which many felt to be an omen boding no good for the future of his enterprise. Recovering himself, however, he rose holding a handful of sand: in his hands, he declared, he held the soil of England. Whether this story is true or not, it was in this way that William interpreted the result of his conquest. He had become lord of the land of England and in future no-one could own land in England any more: they could only hold it from the king.

The basis of all land-holding in England after the Conquest was primarily military. When the fighting ended, William still needed an army to protect his conquest against rebellion by the English or attack from outside. He provided for his needs in the following manner. About 180 'barons' were given varying amounts of land, on condition that they would train about 5,000 'knights' to serve the king in war. These barons were by no means identical with those who had followed William at Hastings, though many of them had been important supporters of his invasion plans. Another 800 knights or thereabouts were to be provided by bishops and abbots, making a total available force of nearly six thousand mailed cavalrymen.

There was, of course, danger in putting so much land into the hands of so few great men, the more so since the training of armed followers was the condition of their holdings. To some extent this danger was lessened, though without any regular design, by the granting of land, not in compact blocks, but in holdings scattered throughout England. Henry Ferrers, the first earl of Derby, for instance, received his main holding in Derbyshire and Leicestershire, where he possessed 114 and 35 lordships respectively, but he also had 20 Berkshire lordships and some land in eleven other counties. The earl of Derby was a large landholder, but the smallest of William's baronies, consisting of as little as nineteen manors, were scattered in the same way as the largest holdings.

Such lordships came to be known as 'manors', from a French

D

word for a dwelling. But a manor was more than a house: it implied a landed estate and the services and rents that the peasants working on that land owed to the lord of the manor. It also involved the idea of a law-court, where he would dispense justice to his peasants. It was not necessarily the same thing as a village, because a village was often divided up among several manors and a manor was often composed of several villages or parts of villages.

The word 'knight' also needs explanation. It originally meant no more than a household servant and this is what, in the first instance, most knights were – quite lowly men, the servants of their lord, living in his hall and sworn to support him in war and, when necessary, to fight for the king. When there was no fighting to be done, their duty was to garrison their lord's castles and, when ordered, the king's, and to act as escorts for their lord. Quite soon, however, they became landholders themselves, for it was inconvenient and expensive for their lord to support them in his house. Thus great barons, who held their wide lands directly from the king, bestowed manors upon their knights on condition that they should hold themselves ready to fight when called upon; and some of these knights, too, divided their lands – granting at least a portion of them to men who would take the burden of fighting off their hands.

There were, however, two parts of England where the holdings of land were not scattered, but kept in compact blocks. These were the borders of Scotland and Wales, where constant insecurity made it necessary to have large forces available for swift action. Thus the prince bishop of Durham was given lands in a compact block and power to raise what was in effect a private army. Similarly, on the borders or 'marches' of Wales, the three great earldoms of Chester, Shrewsbury and Hereford were created by the king, whose holders were expressly excluded from his general prohibition of private warfare. In this way, in succeeding centuries, a very large part of Wales came under the control of the Marcher earls, who placed the widest interpretation upon their role as defenders of the borders of England.

The obligation to provide and train knights for the service of the king fell most hardly upon the bishops and abbots – the ecclesiastical barons of the king, whose main business and enjoyment was not warfare. Anselm, for instance, when archbishop of Canterbury, was accused by William II of failing to train the Canterbury knights and was threatened with retribution in the royal court. Therefore, by the reign of Henry I, it became more and more the custom that church barons could offer money instead of knights to the king – a payment which in later reigns (as we shall see) came to be accepted from other barons as well.

The Claims of the Overlord

In Saxon England loyalty to a man's lord was a real thing, extending if need be to death itself. In the England of the Normans the binding claims of loyalty appear to be as strong, but they are more formal – a matter of law rather than love. The whole inter-locking chain of military obligation was bound together by the twin oaths of homage and fealty. When a baron received land from the king, he knelt before him, put his hands between those of the king, and said 'I become your man'. This was the ceremony of homage, which was followed by that of fealty, when the king's baron (now his 'vassal') laid his hands upon a copy of the gospels and swore to be faithful. The same ceremonies were followed all down the chain of land-holding: lesser men swearing homage and fealty to the lords from whom they held their land, and in turn receiving the oaths from men who held land from them. It was a logical pyramid of obligations, with the king at the apex of it as the overlord of every man.

Yet, in spite of all these interlocking oaths of faithfulness, there might in practice, though not in theory, be a conflict between the loyalty owed by a man to his immediate lord and that he owed to the king: he might be used for private warfare between baron and baron or for actual rebellion. Private wars were formally banned, and to guard against the graver peril of rebellion the Norman kings demanded direct oaths of allegiance from all landholders, whether they held land directly from the king or not. William the Conqueror first demanded the taking of such an oath from the most important sub-tenants at Salisbury near the close of his reign, and it became a principle of law by the time of Henry I.

The main obligation of a landholding vassal to his lord was that of producing knights to fight for him and for the king, but there were lesser rights than this that a lord could insist on. He could claim the payment of a 'relief' from his vassal at the moment he received his lands. This was a form of death duty; the eldest son was accepted as the rightful inheritor of his father's lands, but he had to pay a relief to his lord for the privilege of inheriting. Younger sons had no automatic right to land and had to seek their own fortunes; sometimes they became Crusaders.

It often happened, of course, that estates descended to daughters or to minors. The lord then had the right to control the marriage of the heiress, or to exercise wardship over a minor up to the age of twenty-one – after which the unfortunate heir still had to pay a relief from whatever was left of his estate.

It was also the right of the lord to demand a money 'aid' from his vassals – when, for instance, his eldest son came of age, or his eldest daughter was married, or he himself was held to ransom. A grasping lord, however, could demand aids on many other occasions, at least until Magna Carta limited them in principle to three – and even then the amount was restricted only to what was 'reasonable'. Such rights as these were claimed by all lords, but especially by the king over barons who held land direct from himself; his too energetic exercise of these rights lay behind many of the baronial revolts of the Middle Ages.

It can be seen therefore that loyalty to a lord was a far more cut-and-dried obligation to a Norman than it had been to a Saxon: it was expressed by rights on the one hand and duties on the other. However, not all the rights lay with the lord and the duties with his vassal or tenant: the lord also had duties, which he ignored at his peril. When Henry I came to the throne, he issued a coronation charter, which was confirmed by several of his successors, declaring in detailed terms that he would rule according to law and accepted custom. If he did not do so, the barons would have the charter as a justification for rebellion. There was in fact something of a contract in the medieval idea of lordship. If a lord overworked his rights and oppressed his tenants, they might, at least in theory, renounce their allegiance by a solemn act of 'diffidation' or defiance.

Strength of Norman Kings

England suffered less from this kind of feudal anarchy than many parts of the continent from which her new rulers came. One reason was the compactness of her insular position, which made it relatively easy for them to maintain their authority here while also asserting big claims to territory across the Channel. But it is probably right to attach chief importance to the strong if unattractive characters of William I and most of his early successors. William II, nicknamed Rufus from his apoplectic complexion, was the Conqueror's favourite son and distinguished by his diabolical rages. Henry I, less cruel than his brother, was a warrior first and foremost, but he began the practice of sending out royal officials to make his presence felt in all parts of the country. His long reign was followed, indeed, by the 'nineteen long winters' of Stephen, when protracted civil war enabled the barons to rule their fiefs as tyrannically as they pleased and more than a thousand new castles are said to have been erected without royal permission. But this was remedied by the thorough re-organization of the government by Henry II, a ruler whose energy was matched by his great understanding of affairs; his prestige survived even his association with the murder of archbishop Becket.

For nearly a century after Henry II's death in 1189 the kings of England made a rather smaller direct contribution to the strength of their kingdom. The crusader king, Richard I, spent in England only six months of the ten years of his reign, while his younger brother John is remembered chiefly by his enforced acceptance of Magna Carta, though his reign is also important for another enforced event, namely the separation of England from any connection with Normandy. The long reign of Henry III (1216–1272) is likewise famous above all for his long conflict with the barons under Simon de Montfort, yet a leading modern historian pronounces that Henry 'left England more united, more peaceful, more beautiful than it was when he was a child'.[1] Many failures may be forgiven to the rebuilder of Westminster Abbey, but for the present purpose it is more relevant to point to the

[1] Sir Maurice Powicke: *The Thirteenth Century*, p. 19.

achievements of his son, Edward I, the great law-giver and traditional founder of parliament. As the conqueror of Wales and near-
conqueror of Scotland his name will occur again in a chapter on
warfare, but enough has now been said about rulers and we may
return to the means by which they ruled.

Court and Government

The Anglo–Norman state was probably the most efficient in
Europe, yet its government was simple and almost homely, and
was, in fact, based upon conditions obtaining in a medieval castle.
There the main divisions were the hall, where the lord, whether
king or baron, lived and dined; the chamber, where he slept; the
chapel; and the yard where the horses were kept. In the king's
household, however, the chief officers who took nominal charge of
these divisions were in practice the great barons who served him
in the administration of the whole country.

Presiding over the king's service in the hall were the steward
and the master butler and, over the chamber, the chamberlain
and the treasurer – for in very early times some of the king's
treasure was kept under the royal bed. The chief officer of the
chapel was the chancellor, whose pay was the highest in the king's
service: five shillings a day, three loaves, two measures of wine,
one wax candle and forty candle-ends, together with two meals a
day at the royal expense. The title 'chancellor' comes from the
Latin word *cancella*, meaning a screen, for behind such a screen
the royal clerks sat, separated from the main part of the hall
(rather than the chapel), copying out charters and many other
documents. Finally, the chief officers of the courtyard were the
constables and the marshal, titles with a military ring whose possessors in theory looked after the stables and the kennels and protected the precincts of the palace. Below all these chief officers
there were, of course, lesser men, who did the day-to-day work
about the household.

The king's court was constantly on the move, which meant that
the government moved as well, but it could always be found at
certain fixed places during the great festivals of the year. For
Christmas it was at Gloucester, for Easter at Winchester, and for

Whitsun at Westminster. This meant that everything had to be portable – the luggage of the chapel, for instance, down at least to the reign of John, was carried on two pack-horses. The Treasury and its offshoot the Exchequer, were the only fixed points within this migratory court, for their business soon became so cumbrous and so regular that they could not travel as the court did and became fixed, eventually at Westminster. The Exchequer got its name from a table, marked in squares like a chess-board, on which counters were moved about to represent sums of money, whenever the royal accounts were made up at Easter and Michaelmas. For it was not until the thirteenth century that addition and other types of calculation were simplified by the introduction of Arabic in place of Roman numerals. The summaries of each individual account – that is, largely, of accounts from counties showing the taxes brought in by the sheriffs – were entered upon parchment 'pipes', made up from two sheepskins sewn end to end, which were rolled up to form pipe rolls. One of these remains from the reign of Henry I and an almost unbroken series from that of Henry II – a remarkably detailed record of administration in these early times.

When the court moved to Gloucester, Winchester or Westminster on the occasion of the great Church festivals, it was met by the leading barons who held land directly from the king, and became for a while merged in the 'Great Council' of the king. Any lord in Norman times had both the right and the duty to seek the advice of his vassals; and while these councils, whether of noble or king, were mainly social affairs, they were occasions when important business was also done. It was at the Christmas Great Council in 1085, for instance, that orders went out for the compilation of Domesday Book – a matter that touched all the barons closely.

Nevertheless, the government of England was not conducted through the Great Council but through the royal court or *Curia Regis*, which was sufficiently small and permanent to deal with day-to-day affairs. It was also a law court, even though the majority of its members were not lawyers, and to it appeals came up from shire courts all over the country. Its function was not, however, only to hear appeals: in the reign of Henry I it began to supervise the activities of the shire courts through officials travelling in the royal service. This was only the beginning of a practice which Henry II, in particular, greatly developed, but in it may be discovered the germ of the modern assize courts.

Such was the central government of England after the coming of the Normans and the way in which royal control was exercised through the structure of landholding and military service, the activities of the royal court, and the device of the Great Council. It remains to notice the position of the sheriff.

The Danes had divided the country into great earldoms as a means of governing their conquest. But it was never a very satisfactory method, for these earls did not regard themselves as agents of the king and developed semi-independent powers. Edward the Confessor, for instance, had every reason to fear the power of Harold, earl of Wessex, which threatened the throne itself, and William I, having contested the throne with this earl-turned-king, destroyed almost completely the functions of the Anglo-Danish earldoms, leaving only the title for further use. He relied instead upon a much older Saxon official, the sheriff, who became the main link between the central government and the localities. These sheriffs were members of the baronial class – great men in their own right – and their main functions were to preside over the shire court and to organize the collection of taxes, which they paid into the treasury. But their power, too, tended to become too great and many of them thought of the office as hereditary. From time to time the early Norman kings were forced to dismiss many of them and to replace them by new officials, who often ran the affairs of several counties simultaneously.

Domesday Book

The most striking illustration of the sort of co-operation that went on between the central government of the king and that of the localities is provided by the making of Domesday Book. In the year 1085–1086 William surveyed the country of which he had become king twenty years before. Royal commissioners were sent to each shire to collect, probably in an enlarged meeting of the shire court, details of every manor – who owned it then and before the Conquest, its value at the two dates, its present population, plough teams, and stock. This evidence was obtained from sworn groups of local men – another example of the use of the jury which has already been noticed in the Danelaw. A summary was then compiled in book form, which quickly became known as the Domesday Book, for the strictness of the inquiries suggested the Day of Judgment. There is nothing like it in the early records of any other country; the ability to have such an order carried out within a year shows what power the new monarchy had developed in England.

The Royal Forests

Probably the most unpopular of all Crown activities was the extension of the royal forests.

In the forests [it was said at the time] are the secret places of the kings and their great delight. To them they go for hunting, having put off their cares, so that they may enjoy a little quiet. There, away from the continuous business and incessant turmoil of the court, they can for a little time breathe in the grace of natural liberty, wherefore it is that those who commit offences there lie under the royal displeasure.

Put like this, the royal passion for hunting seems harmless and even idyllic – until it is realized how large an area of the country was occupied by these hunting-grounds, which were not necessarily tree-covered but which had to be left wild as cover for game. It was possible to walk south-westwards from the Thames all the way to the New Forest, which William I created, and never to leave forest land. North of the Thames, it began with Essex, where Epping Forest is a relic of what once covered the whole county; north of the Trent, with Sherwood, which then occupied all the western half of Nottinghamshire. In Yorkshire there were the extensive forests of Galtres and Pickering, and much of the wild country of Northumberland and Cumberland was forest – and this does not exhaust the list.

Within these forests, the beasts which were the objects of Norman hunting – the red, fallow and roe deer and the wild boar –

were protected against poaching by savage penalties. These were inflicted in the forest courts, to whose officials the people who lived within the boundaries of the forests were specially answerable. To poach a deer from the royal forests put life or limb at peril, and no dog could be kept there unless three talons were cut from each of its paws. It was not only the game that was protected – but also the timber, which could not be cut without permission, and the land itself, which could not be ploughed up. This was in spite of the fact that whole villages lay within the boundaries of such forests, which were declared to be royal forests by the king's will alone.

Castle Building

If, in the country, the forests and their French laws were felt to be a savage reminder of the fact of Norman conquest, in the towns it was the looming menace of the castle that reminded men of their new masters. In the earliest days of the conquest, the interests of king and baron were the same – the holding of what they had won, not so much against each other as against the English people. William I embarked upon a wide programme of castle building and the royal castles went up in all the county towns, the sheriff of the county in many cases being put in charge of them as the royal 'castellan'. But barons, too, were encouraged to build castles in the centres where their main estates lay and to install their own castellans within them. The royal castles, and the baronial ones also, were garrisoned by the knights whom king or baron raised – performing their duties of 'castle-guard'. But from the beginning, in order to insure against too great baronial independence, William insisted that he had a right to garrison baronial castles himself upon demand. Under these conditions, therefore, the royal and baronial castles mushroomed throughout England, until, by 1100, there were five or six thousand of them.

This number may seem a surprisingly large one, if one has in mind the more complex castles of a later date. But the earliest Norman castles were of the simplest type: that at York, for instance, is believed to have gone up in eight days, and there were a good many which occupied only a single acre of ground. They consisted simply of an artificial mound or 'motte', crowned by a wooden palisade and surrounded by a ditch. This was adjoined by a lower and larger defended area, the 'bailey', which was likewise surrounded by a ditch and palisade. There was usually a wooden tower on the motte, and the bailey contained wooden buildings to house the garrison and their horses.

In these early days there were no stone towers built on the mounds – a fact which is accounted for both by the necessity for speed in their erection and the difficulty in obtaining sufficient stone; in any case, a newly raised mound could not have taken any heavy stone superstructure with safety. In time, however, the wooden palisades were replaced by stone, so that there developed the type of Norman castle known as a 'shell-keep'. A little later, however, this gave way to the better-known square keeps, two of which – the White Tower in the Tower of London and the huge keep at Colchester – date from the eleventh century. The development can be marked, for instance, at Guildford, where the remains of the earlier shell-keep can be seen on the mound below the later square tower. Within this sort of tower, though never on the ground floor, were the main rooms of the lord's household: the great hall, with the chamber of the lord either branching off it or on a higher floor, and the chapel.

What Survived in England

Forest law and castle were constant reminders to Englishmen of their subject status, but an even more potent indication of this lay in the disappearance of their language from educated usage. The new rulers of England spoke Norman–French, of which many of their subjects perforce acquired a smattering; this situation, coupled with the use of Latin in the services of the church and in all legal and administrative written business, drove the English language underground for at least two hundred years. Nevertheless, the various dialects of Old English did not die out but continued to be used probably by a majority of the nation, though they developed in spoken rather than written forms. Yet it would be wrong to separate them too rigidly from the Norman–French of the governing classes, which exercised a strong and constant influence upon their vocabulary and even their grammar. The

Norman–French cleric speaks to us in such words as 'chaplain', 'miracle', 'paradise', and 'saint'; the lay official in 'court', 'crown', 'council', and 'justice'; the military in 'standard', 'tower', 'treason', 'peace' and 'war'. The English language survived, but it was modified and enriched by the inclusion of words long heard from the lips of a foreign master.

To end on such a note – of the gulf between the conquered English and their new rulers – may seem to imply that the Normans ignored altogether the traditions of the English and governed with nothing but Norman precedents in mind: that the Norman conquest was similar, at least in this way, to the Roman. This would be quite wrong: the old English kingdom was already well developed and the Normans borrowed from its experience in countless ways. Government by the king's court may be said to hark back to the Saxon institution of the Witan; the sheriff is in origin a Saxon official; the shire itself and the shire court are Saxon institutions; and the liberties of Englishmen, which Norman kings guaranteed at their coronation, were those accepted by Edward the Confessor – the list could be extended almost indefinitely. Yet it is true that into the place of the old English governing class the new Norman one stepped, usurping their social position and their lands: they had both ousted their predecessors and depressed their status. Herein lay what may fairly be called the social revolution of 1066.

Wales and Scotland

Both Wales and Scotland, as we might expect, found the Norman kings of England more determined than their predecessors to assert the claims to suzerainty which had existed at least since the time of Edgar. Perhaps it was chiefly the poverty of Wales which deterred the Marcher lords from pushing their conquests farther than they did – they were more interested in winning land for themselves on the continent. In spite of several full-scale invasions, rather more than half of modern Wales remained in the possession of its native princes; in 1267 Llywelyn, grandson of an often victorious North Welsh ruler of the same name, was given treaty recognition as 'prince of Wales'. But the onward move of Norman civilization was marked nevertheless by the foundation of the diocese of St David's, in the occupied territory of the south-west, and by the spread of Cistercian abbeys into many moorland valleys.

Anglo–Scottish relations involved military conflicts on less unequal terms. William II wrested control of Cumberland from the Scots, but this and much of the north were temporarily lost again in the time of Stephen, in spite of a notable English victory at the battle of the Standard, where the shire levies rallied behind the banners of their patron saints. Although the Scots did not finally abandon their claim to the northern counties until 1237, border quarrels were in the long run less important than the peaceful penetration of the Norman way of life into the whole of the lowland area north of the border.

Much was due to the influence of St Margaret, a grand-niece of Edward the Confessor. She became the mother of three Scottish kings, including David I who was brought up largely at the court of Henry I. From the beginning of his reign in 1124 may be dated the settlement of many Norman barons in southern Scotland, the building of castles and abbeys, and the organization of central and local government on feudal lines. The Highlands, however, and Galloway in the south-west with its separate laws, remained largely unaffected by the new style of centralized royal government. Nor did the new régime as yet have strength to wrest from Norway the sovereignty of the isles and the two mainland counties of Caithness and Sutherland.

MEDIEVAL ENGLISH SOCIETY

7

LIFE ON THE MANOR

IN the last chapter we saw how the greater and lesser barons received land, whether directly or indirectly, from the king in return for military service and how the holdings of land they received were called manors. We have looked at this system, so to speak, from on top: now we have to look at it from the underside – from the view of a peasant working on a manor and subject to a lord. From the start, however, there is a complication: a peasant might work under very different conditions according to where he lived. The typical 'manorial system' is in fact typical only in the south and midlands. Outside this area, and in Wales and most of Scotland, other ways of organizing farming were dominant. Some attention will be paid to these, but in the main it is the southern and the midland peasant who is the subject of this chapter.

In a sense the manorial system of the early middle ages appears under false pretences: it poses as something new, while in fact it is very old. The word 'manor' first appears in England in 1067, but the thing it represents is much older. In Saxon times the peasants already farmed strips in the open fields and many of them had lords. The Normans introduced no new method of farming, but they did emphasize in quite a new way the legal side of the manor – the relationship between a peasant and his lord.

View of a Manorial Village

From the top of a hill it might easily have been possible to see the whole of a typical manor stretched out below and, on a still day, to hear its noises – peasant shouting in the fields, the bellowing of cattle, and perhaps the clatter of a mill-wheel by the stream. From the hill, the houses would stand out clearly. Some of them were no better than shacks, floorless, walled with intertwined wattle made solid by clay, and topped by a crudely thatched roof. They would perhaps have no more than a single unglazed window and only a hole in the roof to act as a chimney. Part of the house would be used as a stable, for most villagers had two or three cattle to keep, and as a hen-roost too. The houses usually faced on to a rough street, but did not line it quite in the manner of later village houses, for each cottage was surrounded by its own garden, though the main part lay to the back, away from the street. Here, separately from the routine of the crops in the fields, the peasant could grow his own vegetables and keep bees, which were then the only source of sugar. Probably most of the vegetables were simple enough, though many varieties were known. There were cabbages, turnips, lettuces, leeks and onions, and also garlic, pumpkins and cucumbers. There were fruits, too, grown perhaps in small orchards, among which apples, pears, plums and cherries would be the most common. In the early middle ages, there were even attempts to grow vines for wine – until the development of trade with France showed how hopeless it was to try and compete with sunnier climates.

Our imaginary watcher from the hill could trace the line of the dusty street – which often keeps its original shape – where the thin dogs snarled and fought, until it reached the centre of the village and a wooden enclosure where some cattle endlessly chewed and stamped. This was the 'pound', where villagers' beasts which had strayed into the open fields, or had been withheld by their owners from the lord's service, were detained (their owners having to feed them meantime) until the lord released them.

Near to the pound, in the centre of the village, stood the church – the only stone building apart from the manor-house, and perhaps boasting a new, squat Norman tower. Probably its churchyard lay to the south of it, for this was widely regarded as the side which received light and warmth from the fellowship of the saints: when the priest read the gospel at Mass, he turned to the north, towards the darkness and cold where the words were most needed. Inside the dimly lit building, the walls glowed with a more pictorial gospel – portraying the joys of heaven and the pains of hell. Here too, outside the times of worship, the villagers met to discuss all sorts of village business.

Very near to the church, our watcher would see the manor-house with its thick stone walls and small round-headed windows – halfway between a castle and a house, turning its back on the village and looking into its interior courtyard. Together with its barns and stables, it might be surrounded by a moat and probably also by some enclosed farming land, quite distinct from the village fields. This was part of the lord's 'demesne' – that portion of the land that he kept for his own use. The rest of it would fairly certainly be mixed up with the lands of the peasants in the great open fields. The lord of the manor would not live in the house the whole year round. He would probably be lord of more manors than one, and would spend the greater part of the year visiting them and living off the food his bailiff had collected for him, both from the demesne and from the enforced gifts of his peasants. The bailiff lived on the manor permanently: he was the representative of the lord and ran the manor in his absence.

The Open Fields

To the modern eye, however, the most striking feature of the manor would be none of the things so far described but rather the spreading vastness of its two or three fields, undivided by hedge or permanent fence. In a few places in England even today there are survivals of such fields: at Laxton in Nottinghamshire the south field is 500 acres in extent. This, then, is the sort of field that we must picture. Manors with three great fields predominated eventually in midland and southern England, and it seems likely that on heavy soils the use of three rather than two fields was beginning to be imitated from continental practice about the time of the Norman Conquest. Thus wheat or rye was sown in autumn; barley or oats in spring; and the third field lay fallow, with two ploughings in early summer. If there were only two fields, they might be sown in halves. In either case, an annual rotation of fields left a large part of the arable soil unused each year, in order to restore its fertility.

But in western and northern districts, where the relatively infertile land needed longer than a year to regain its growing powers, a different system prevailed. In this case the in-field, which would probably be the land nearest to the village, would bear the whole year's crops of wheat, oats, barley and peas – even though some would be sown in spring and others in autumn. The outfield would then consist of almost the whole of the remaining land, including some parts, such as swamps and woods, which obviously could not be ploughed. But the better parts of the outfield would be used piecemeal, bits being ploughed up and cropped as required and then allowed to revert to rough pasture. Ultimately, however, the growth of population might result in the carving-up of the out-field, so as to provide a second permanent field, and at that stage some regular rotation of crops would probably be introduced.

Apart from the great size of these unfenced fields, the method of ploughing them would be of immediate interest to a modern observer. They were ploughed in separate strips, which could vary in size between a quarter and a full acre. At their largest they were 22 yards broad and 220 yards long: a standard length whatever the size of the strip, so far as the lie and quality of the land allowed it. Such strips made up the holdings of the peasants and they were widely scattered throughout the two or three fields. To watch a plough-team of four – or occasionally, on virgin or very heavy soil, eight – oxen at work on one of these strips would suggest a reason for their standard length. Ploughing required a mixture of skill, experience and brute strength, and to cajole and control so many uneasily yoked animals was something no novice could attempt. As many as four men might be at work on the job: one, the ploughman himself, holding and steering the plough; another to goad and encourage the oxen, walking backwards in front of them; another to plod beside the plough, adjusting the plough beam and helping to guide it; and perhaps another to ride on the plough to weight it down and keep it steady in the ground. So ploughing was a matter of shouting and struggle – men against beasts and both against the soil. In these circumstances 220 yards (a furlong or furrow-long) was about the farthest that the oxen could be goaded to go without demanding a rest from straining against the yoke. Since a rest could be combined with the turn it was common sense to make the turn at that point. But turning was a waste of effort and therefore ploughmen did as little of it as possible – they made the furrows as long as they could, only turning when they had to: this settled the length of the strip.

Since this length was more or less fixed, differences in the size of the strip could only come from the width, and this varied between 5½ yards and the 22 already noticed. Yet the strips were not rigidly rectangular but took on rather the curving outline of a long 'S'. The ploughman would swing the oxen outwards as he approached the end of the furrow, in order to make the turn easier, and this provided the strips with the shape that experts call the 'aratral curve'.

In a large open field of, say, 500 acres, the next thing to be remarked would be the way in which the strips were made up into blocks. These were known as 'furlongs', which is a confusing term because for us it represents only a length – and has already been used in this sense here. In the middle ages, however, it could also mean an area, one side of which was fairly well defined as 220 yards; the other being much less definite, depending on how many strips were put into the block. This seems a strange method of organization unless it is realized that these great open fields had very seldom been brought initially into cultivation all at one go – they were made up bit by bit, as land was won from the surrounding waste. Since nearly every household in the village might take a share in the winning of the land and expect to be rewarded, strips in each new 'furlong' would be shared out piece-meal among the villagers concerned. Custom might, for instance, prescribe that the village priest received the end strip in every furlong in the field.

The spacious look of the great undivided open fields has already been remarked – though it might be imagined that the many and separate strips of the peasants within them would lead to more rather than less numerous divisions. But these strips were separated by no more than narrow pieces of unploughed grass, and even the furlongs were divided in the same way. The only fencing in use was temporary – put up to protect the whole field rather than the individual strips from straying cattle during the growing period of the crops. After harvest this was removed and the cattle were allowed to graze in the long stubble. Yet the fields did not look as uniform as might be expected: only the furrows ran predominantly the same way, parallel with each other, within the furlong block. So the fields presented a patch-work appearance, which was further broken up by occasional areas unfit for ploughing.

Within these open fields lay the total holding of the peasant – whom we should now begin to call a 'villein', though the term will have to be explained later.[1] The total of his arable holding was known as a 'virgate' or 'yardland', traditionally thirty acres but in practice a very variable amount. But whether a particular virgate was one of ten acres or eighty, it always represented a considerable number of strips: a villein was by no means a landless man.

Meadow, Pasture, and Waste

Beside the river could be seen the lush meadow lands – in many ways the most valuable part of the manor, providing the best means by which cattle could be maintained through the winter. On the success of the hay harvest depended how large a part of the stock would have to be slaughtered in the autumn. Great efforts would be made to keep in good fettle the draught animals that pulled the plough, but at Michaelmas most of the others would have to go, providing more meat than any manor could use at one moment. Most of it was preserved in salt – a commodity in constant demand and traded all over the country. So the meadows were valued highly and protected carefully. Like the arable fields, they were divided into strips but, unlike them, they were often allocated by lot and shared out afresh each year.

In the arable fields, except through special circumstances, the strips were never altered and were passed down from father to son. From 2nd February (Candlemas) to 1st August (Lammas) the

[1] See p. 93

fields were closed by temporary fences; but in August, when the harvest was complete, they were thrown open to the cattle of the whole manor, the strips being disregarded till the next season. This grazing of sheep and cattle, whether upon arable or meadow land (the latter opened in July, as soon as the hay harvest was in) did more than merely feed the animals on the long stubble left by medieval sickles – it fed the land, too. The use of manure in farming was well understood, and one of the many obligations that the villein owed his lord was the putting out of his sheep on enclosed demesne land to manure it. But the lord also had his strips in the meadows and numerous strips belonging to his demesne in each of the great fields of the manor.

Surrounding the ploughed fields, the meadows and the village itself, there was always the woodland and other 'waste' – rough ground that had not yet been ploughed up and perhaps could not be. This tangle of waste and woodland divided manor from manor. Yet it was shrinking year by year, to meet the needs of a growing population, even though the passion for hunting of king and baron held up the process. In this waste land the peasants were allowed to turn their pigs and geese loose to forage for themselves and could collect turves and firewood – the latter defined as branches dead enough to be pulled down with a hook.

Population Free and Unfree

It is time now to consider who these villeins and other inhabitants of the manor were. There is no doubt that they fell into two main classes, the free and the unfree. Although there were occasionally exceptional groups whom we might describe as half-free, the position of a free man was usually distinctive in three respects. Firstly, he paid rent for his land rather than rendering services to his lord for it – though, even so, he was not entirely exempt from such services. Secondly, he could sell his land if he wished and leave the manor. Thirdly, he had the right to sue in matters concerning his tenement in the royal courts, whereas the unfree could only do so in the court of the manor.

The freemen were very much of a minority group on a typical Norman manor. For the most part they were persons who paid rent for a substantial holding of land. But they might also hold less land than a villein – or possibly none at all, in which case they worked for wages or, more probably, made their living by some handicraft, as millers, blacksmiths, potters, or wheelwrights.

Turning back to the unfree majority, we may begin by noticing briefly a group about which we hear much less than its numbers warrant. Slavery disappeared very rapidly after the Norman Conquest, though there are still many slaves recorded in Domesday Book, especially on the borders of Wales. Some of them probably became manorial servants in direct dependence on the lord, such as the ploughmen he required to supplement the work of the villeins on his demesne land. In general, however, the slaves were replaced at the very bottom of the social pyramid by 'cottars' or 'bordars', people who had much less land than a villein and owed correspondingly fewer services to the lord. Sometimes they were known as 'Monday-men', which implies that from Tuesday to Saturday they must eke out a living by doing whatever odd jobs were available, either for the lord or for the more prosperous villeins. In bad seasons they and their families would be the first to starve.

Most unfree persons, however, belonged to families of villein status, of which the head held a virgate of land in the open fields and was in practice allowed to pass it on from father to son. Yet he was not free: he could not leave the manor as a freeman could, and he was bound to perform a whole range of services to his lord in return for the land he held. He was not even considered to be entirely responsible for his own actions, but was grouped with nine or eleven others in what were known as 'tithings' or 'frankpledges', each member of which had to be answerable for the good behaviour of the rest: freeholders were exempt from this.

Yet it was always possible for a villein to become free, and there were at least four ways in which this could be done. Firstly, he might buy his freedom from the lord – which was difficult to do unless he had some means of making money. Secondly, he might change – or 'commute' – his labour services on the land for rent. Commutation existed as early as the twelfth century, but (as we shall see in a later chapter)[1] its extent fluctuated in accordance

[1] See p. 155

with the interests of the lords: it was not a privilege on which the peasant could count. Thirdly, there was the chance of escape. If a villein could get to a chartered borough and live there for a year and a day without being caught, he would gain his freedom. Finally, he could become a priest – though he would have to get permission from his lord to do so. So the walls round a villein were not impossibly high to climb, but everything depended on whether it paid his lord to keep him hemmed in.

Obligations of a Villein

The most important of the services that a villein had to do for his lord was 'week-work'. This consisted of two or three days' work a week upon the lord's demesne, for which villein services provided the bulk of the labour. This was not in fact so great a burden as it may sound: only one person from each villein's family had to go and it would have been foolish to have sent the best worker. Ploughing usually stopped at midday and, if it went on longer, the lord might have to provide the villein's food. The villein in his turn, however, had to lend a beast or two for the ox-team. But ploughing was not the only job to be done – there was carting, sheep-shearing, upkeep of buildings, land clearance, and many other kinds of estate work.

At the busiest seasons, such as the hay or corn harvest, the villein would be required to do 'boon-work' at the lord's demand. This was something over and above the regular services and even freemen might have to do it. A boon is a gift and there was about boon-work something of the idea that it was freely given by the peasants, which was probably why freemen had to do it when asked and certainly why the lord always fed the workers on a boon day. Bread, beer and herrings did something to lighten the burden for these not too willing workers.

Most manors had a watermill or (later) a windmill, owned by the lord. Here the villeins were forced to bring their corn to be ground and to pay for the privilege, and on some manors they had to bring their bread to be baked in the lord's oven. At Easter they had to make a gift of eggs to the lord – from which custom the modern Easter egg comes down. All these services and obligations, although burdensome, were at least regular and expected. But there were others, equally hard, which came suddenly upon the villein with little warning: Such was the 'heriot' tax – a form of death duty – which a villein's heir had to pay to the lord before he could take over the virgate. The amount of it was a matter for the lord's bailiff: if there were more than three beasts, then the best of them might be taken; if less, then some article such as a cooking pot from the house. And there was the humiliating 'merchet' tax, to be paid when the daughter of a villein was married.

All this reveals the manor as a highly complex organization, one that could never run itself. If a lord had several manors, their administration would be in the hands of a steward who managed the accounts with a staff of clerks and auditors. Below him, the resident representative of the lord on a single manor was the bailiff, who usually ran the manor court and collected the fines imposed there. The day-to-day supervision of the work of the manor and of the performance of all labour services was also the bailiff's job, though he was helped in it by the 'reeve'. The latter was himself a villein, elected annually each autumn by his fellows and relieved from week-work during the period of his office. All livestock and crops had to be carefully accounted for, and barns, carts and ploughs kept in good repair. In all this the bailiff and reeve would work together, providing in themselves a bridge that united the two extremes of manorial society – the bailiff listening to the urgings of the lord and the reeve to the complaints of the villeins. Yet the reeve on his part was not entirely alone: he had the help of specialized officials such as the shepherd, hayward and bee-keeper.

The centre of the organization of the manor was the manor court, held every six weeks in the hall of the manor house and compulsorily attended by the freemen and the villeins together. The bailiff normally presided, unless the steward was there, when he would do so, the bailiff then upholding the cause of the lord and acting as prosecutor. Sentence would be pronounced by the presiding official, but only after the person accused had been found guilty by the freemen and villeins present in the court. By no means all the business was criminal and none of it concerned major crimes, which only the royal courts were allowed to try.

The most usual criminal charges were for such things as petty thefts – and assaults like the following:

> the wife of Gilbert Vicar's son . . . unlawfully struck Hugh of Stanbridge and dragged him by his hair out of his own proper house, to his damage 40s. and to his dishonour 20s.

But most typical of the cases tried by the manor court were those dealing with strictly manorial business – the neglect of week-work, trespassing in the corn, keeping wheat back from the lord's mill, diverting a stream and so forth – things that concerned every land-holder present. For the rest, the business of the court was straight-forward administration – electing the reeve and many of the other manor officials, checking that all the villeins were grouped in tithings, and recording the customary services and gifts that each villein owed his lord. If a copy of an individual record were given to a man, he was said to hold his land by 'copyhold' and could appeal to the record against new obligations suddenly imposed.

Other Systems of Farming

All that has been said so far concerns only the manorial system as it developed in the south and the midlands of England – in a band of land running from the centre of the south coast, up through the midlands; finally curving to the Humber estuary and the north-east coast. It was the area where the Saxon and Norman systems of farming combined to produce the system we have already considered. Outside it, however, different patterns developed out of differing geographical and historical conditions. To the west and north – that is, in Cornwall, Wales, the north-west of England and Scotland – the geographical conditions are such that arable farming is not so easily practised as in the manorial area: the land is high and comparatively barren and the climate more cloudy and wet. It is pasture country rather than arable. Celtic rather than Saxon traditions prevailed, and to much of it the Saxon practice of open-field farming never penetrated. The villages show a difference from those of the central system: farming even today is carried on round scattered homesteads rather than closely knit villages.

In Cornwall and Wales there was little open-field farming, except in Pembrokeshire, and little rotation of crops on the midland pattern – pastoral farming was the main thing. To some extent this was true of Scotland too, though arable crops were grown in Lowland areas such as the Lothians. There the tenants held their lands in separated strips, called 'rigs', of roughly the same size as the English ones. The crops were rotated to some extent but there was no fallow period, regular manuring being relied upon to do the same job. In the Highlands farming was mainly pastoral, though some small-scale arable was practised in the valleys, where land was periodically taken in from the hillsides and cultivated before being allowed to go back to pasture again.

For special reasons East Anglia and Kent provide the final exceptions to the midland manorial pattern. In much of East Anglia the background was Danish, and the Danish tradition was of far greater personal freedom than elsewhere in Britain. The original settlers had been free warriors following leaders whom they came to recognize as their lords, giving them help at such times as harvest and sheep-shearing: but they remained free men and were never bound to the soil as were the villeins to the west of them. Kent also had a nucleus of substantial freemen from the time of the Jutish immigration. In addition, it had a specialized agriculture already centred on fruit-growing, and was in the most economically advanced part of the country, lying across the trade routes to the continent; so labour services came quite early to be replaced by rents and wages.

Importance of Sheep

Only one side of rural life remains to be touched on – the raising of sheep. All men were involved in this, from the lord to the villein, for the sheep had unrivalled uses in the medieval world. The shepherd was already a key-figure at the beginning of the eleventh century, when he figures in Aelfric's *Colloquy*, our oldest English school-book.

First thing in the morning I drive my sheep to pasture and stand over them in heat and cold with dogs lest wolves should devour them, and I lead them back to their sheds and milk them twice a day and move their folds besides, and I make cheese and butter and am faithful to my lord.

Alive, the sheep provided wool, milk, cheese and manure for the land it grazed on; dead, it gave meat and parchment – it was a rich agricultural investment. Of the various breeds in England two stood out – the small, mountain type which produced a short wool with a high felting quality and was found at its best on the Welsh border; and the larger, long-haired type, which produced its finest wool in the Cotswolds, Leicestershire and East Anglia. This lush wool was the envy of the whole of Europe and foreign merchants travelled great distances to buy it. Big landlords, especially ecclesiastical ones, became more and more concerned with the foreign market and built up huge flocks of sheep. As early as 1086 the abbey of Ely maintained 13,400 sheep, and not much later the bishop of Winchester was keeping 29,000. By the thirteenth century even the villeins were beginning to send their wool to market and to know the feel of money as a regular part of life. But sheep-breeding on a large scale could hardly be carried on within the framework of a typical manor, with its strict apportionment of labour services and steady routine of corn-growing. However, a group of manors might be organized to do the job, if they were subject to one lord and near to one another. The bishop of Winchester's flocks, for instance, were raised on his large group of manors in Hampshire. But however the sheep were maintained, they did more than any other single thing to draw England into the main stream of European trade.

Town and country have always influenced each other, passing on their distress or prosperity impartially. As the manors became richer, they sold their surplus corn and wool in the town markets and fairs, where they fetched prices which had a strong influence on manorial life. In the thirteenth century the demand for manorial products rose with the rise in population and prices reached their height. Both lords and villeins therefore did their work with an eye to what went on in the towns. In the next chapter we, too, must look in that direction.

8

THE GROWTH OF TRADE AND TOWNS

THE main provincial towns in the middle ages were not those that loom largest today – such as Birmingham or Glasgow. But some towns may still be found which retain much of their medieval structure and atmosphere. At York, for example, the city centre at least is still much like a town of that time. To enter by its northern gate, Bootham Bar, through the long circuit of the walls, and go past the Minster, through the narrow Shambles, down to the castle and the waterfront by the bridge over the Ouse, is to touch all the essential elements of a medieval town and to breathe much of its atmosphere. For the vital features of any town of the middle ages were its defences, its connection with the Church, its market, its close links with the king or some other lord, and its communications with the outside world.

Layout of a Medieval Town

The walls of York are two and three-quarter miles long and are cut into at various points by massive gates, which connected the ancient city with the country beyond. They certainly presented a formidable obstacle to any enemy for, high enough in themselves, they are for the most part built upon a huge earthen mound and surrounded by a deep moat. The labour required to build such walls was very great; it was one of the duties of every townsman to help with their maintenance.

The primary purpose of the walls of course was defence, for many towns, especially those of Alfred the Great and of Danish England, originated in this primary need – but it was rarely the first purpose of the town itself, which was concentrated upon trade. The walls were useful because they protected the trade carried on within them. They were useful too because they marked out beyond question the boundaries of town government, drawing a line between residents and non-residents, between those who could claim town privileges and those who could not. The gates, closed between sunset and sunrise, were not only designed for exclusion – they were intended, even more importantly, to control the admission of, and payment of toll by, all outsiders who came to town to buy and sell.

The main disadvantage of a walled town was that its growth was restricted. In most towns there was originally space for gardens and orchards, but this was gradually eaten away by the growing population until by the end of the twelfth century every town of importance was overflowing its bounds and flooding beyond the walls. Inside the walls the streets became more and more narrow and the houses more crowded, so that it is perhaps a wonder that the inhabitants did not readily emigrate to the spaces outside. There was, however, much value in being able to claim the full privileges of a townsman or burgess, which only clearly came from the possession of a house within the walls. Narrow streets, such as the Shambles in York or many of those rebuilt on ancient sites within the City of London, give a very good idea of the enforced intimacy of medieval town life. Yet it must be remembered that in Norman times even the bigger provincial towns, such as Norwich, Lincoln, Bristol and York itself, had populations of only four or five thousand. The average town was very much smaller, especially in the north of the island: as late as the beginning of the fourteenth century Berwick's population was about 1,500 and Edinburgh contained no more than four hundred houses.

Agriculture, of course, was by far the most important occupation in the middle ages and even townsmen were not cut off from the land. Outside the town, beyond the walls, there were arable and pasture fields in which most townsmen had a share – though as free men, not closely tied to lords of manors in the country round. Nevertheless, the lords who held sway beyond the town area often retained a close interest in its affairs. Many towns had been founded by barons on their own estates, and they often contained the town houses of neighbouring manorial lords. In such a way a lord of a manor gained the right to sell his surplus produce in the town market and was free from toll. He also had a place of safety within the walls and, if the town were a county town, a convenient residence during the meetings of the shire court which, as a great man of the shire, he would have to attend. So the lives of town and country were not separate in those days but closely interwoven.

The part that the Church played in town life was considerable. The earliest markets were held in churchyards and usually on Sundays, when the parishioners attended service and so were at hand for trading. Fairs, too, were often held on the day, or during the week, of the festival of the patron saint. Papal opposition, however, to this worldly connection between parish churches and town markets grew in the thirteenth century, and Edward I's Statute of Winchester demanded that 'henceforth neither fairs nor markets be kept in churchyards for the honour of the Church'. Yet the market-place was rarely far from the church, and in monastic boroughs it was usually just outside the abbey gate.

At every point the life of the Church touched that of the town. When craft organizations began to develop, they commonly had their own patron saints and special chapels within the parish church. Traders coming to the town would often enter it through a gate with a chapel attached, dedicated to the use of travellers, and would never be far from a church building. The sheer number of churches, in fact, coupled with the immense size of the largest of them, suggests another aspect of the impact the church made upon town life – in the employment of labour. Monasteries, cathedrals, and smaller churches too, required the constant services of masons, glaziers, tilers, carpenters and plumbers and, in a time of building or rebuilding, a host of unskilled labourers as well. Their material demands led to further employment far beyond their immediate localities – in the Northamptonshire stone quarries of Barnack, for example, or in the Derbyshire lead mines. Two miles of lead-piping for the abbey of Bury St Edmunds, or the lead-sheeting for the roof of Winchester Cathedral, made great demands on men and supplies of material. And all over Britain by land and water these resources were explored. In 1100 the monks of Durham ordered the casting of a great bell in London, which was laboriously transported to Durham, as many as twenty-two oxen being required to pull it along.

At the outset of this chapter a walk through York was suggested as bringing to one's notice all the main features of a medieval town. Starting with the walls at Bootham Bar, the proposed route would take us next to the Minster and now it leads on to the Shambles, originally the stalls where meat was sold; here even today the houses reach towards each other across the narrow street. This was the centre of the market area and was itself occupied largely by butchers. Next to it there was another market in the street known as 'Pavement', and there was still another known as the 'Thursday Market'. In the later Middle Ages even more developed – a butter market in Micklegate and fishmongers' booths along the riverside. The Shambles is in the heart of the medieval city – and the market was the heart of every town.

Markets and Merchant Gilds

The right of a town to possess a market was eagerly sought after, and in the first instance it could only be granted by the king. He might however, usually for a fee, delegate the right to a lay or spiritual lord to found a market upon his own lands. The pressures upon the king to authorize markets must have been very great, for in the thirteenth century there were 3,000 authorizations granted. Yet the king was paid for granting the market and the towns were rewarded for running it, so that both parties were content. The profits to the town lay in the rents for stalls and shops and the tolls levied on the goods brought in by outsiders for sale, as well as on the activities of brokers who sometimes brought buyer and seller together, and on the use of the town's standard weights and measures.

The running of the market was often in the hands of a body called the Merchant Gild, of which, in the early days at least, any burgess who paid an entrance fee and swore an oath of loyalty could be a member. Only gildsmen were free from tolls in the market and in many places they alone were entitled to sell goods retail. The gild elected their own officers, of whom the chief was the 'alderman', and made rules – which they had the power to enforce by suspension from trading – for the weekly market. Two of the most serious offences were 'forestalling' and 'regrating': the first was stopping sellers on their way to the market so as to buy up their goods beforehand, and the second was the buying of goods in the market in order to sell them again at a higher price.

The officers of the Merchant Gild came to be the same as those of the town – though the chief citizen was known, not by the title of alderman but by the Norman name of mayor (in Scotland, provost). London probably led the way, when in 1191 it set up Henry Fitz Ailwin as its first mayor.

It has already been remarked that York had at least three market-places – and later on, more than this. Lincoln had separate markets for corn, meat, fish, poultry, cloth and skins. Ipswich was a town which had three markets – for butter (the buttermarket is still there, in name at least), timber, and wool – and many towns had two. These markets were not usually held in special market squares. In Oxford both the street called Cornmarket and the Broad Street at right angles to it were markets – the latter for the sale of horses. The wide main street, too, was often a market-place, as at Burford in the Cotswolds. Chelmsford had a triangular market-place, with the church at the base and the river bridge at the apex – and this can still be noticed today in spite of some encroaching building. But many built-over sites of markets are now identifiable only with the help of air photographs.

Most markets were occupied by temporary booths rather than shops, and the town or the merchant gild profited by letting out space for such booths in the street. Medieval shops never kept large stocks, many articles being made on the premises as they were ordered. The shops therefore were often very small, having perhaps no more than a six-foot frontage on the street. Shopkeepers following a particular trade tended to congregate together, so that certain streets came to be centres for particular tradesmen – such as fishmongers and the butchers, already mentioned, of the Shambles in York. The narrow streets had no side pathways and were sloped towards a central gulley, where rubbish lay and rotted.

Fire and disease were among the most frequently met hazards of medieval life.

The Great Fairs

Connected with the market, but not necessarily held on the same site, were the great fairs, where much of the inland as well as overseas trade was carried on, because except at fairtime the traders of even a neighbouring town were liable to the same hindrances as foreigners. The right to hold a market did not include that of organizing a fair, which had to be sought from the king and paid for separately. In any case, most towns were unsuitable as centres for fairs, because they made no pretence of selling to more than their immediate neighbourhood. The right place for a fair was a town which was the natural centre for the trade of a wide area – preferably one which specialized in some article in wide demand – and it needed to have easy communications, particularly with eastern and southern ports.

Whereas markets were normally weekly occasions, most fairs were held annually, and the early practice of choosing Sunday for a market day is paralleled by the frequent choice of a church festival

Plate 15. *Field Strips at Padbury, Bucks.* To recreate the ancient open fields here, the hedges must be ignored and other boundaries looked for. The most obvious is the stream, seen above the lowest hedge in the picture. This separated the furlongs (or blocks of strips) in the open fields: above it, one running towards the top left corner where there still is an unploughed track and, below it, another furlong running off at the bottom edge. (The land immediately above the stream was probably too wet to plough.) The strips of the lower furlong, while parallel with each other, are not in the same alignment as those in the upper one, as was frequently the case with adjacent furlongs. That these ridges and furrows are in fact remains of the open field strips at Padbury is confirmed by a map of 1591; this identifies the possessors of the strips at that date. (Cf. text pp. 88–90.)

Plate 16. *Broadcast Sowing.* Sowing by throwing the grain haphazardly over the ploughed and harrowed soil: a method of immemorial antiquity, described with all its drawbacks in the New Testament Parable of the Sower (Mark iv. 3–8), and not improved upon until the invention of the seed drill in Britain in the eighteenth century. (Cf. text pp. 88–9.)

Plate 17. *The Shambles, York.* This gives a good idea of the appearance of a medieval street, with the houses crowded within the confining walls of the town – though, in fact, nothing in the Shambles is older than Tudor and early Stuart times. (Cf. text pp. 100, 102, 103.)

Plate 15

semen huiu iacto

Plate 16

Plate 17

for the holding of a fair. The fair at St Ives (Hunts), for instance, was held in Easter week and that at Gloucester began on the Eve of St John the Baptist's Day. There was no one length accepted as the time a fair should run: that at Gloucester was for five days, while Winchester's started at three days but was later extended to fourteen and finally to twenty-four. The longer the fair, of course, the greater the profits that might be made from it – in rents and tolls and fines from the fair court. This was sometimes called the court of 'pie-powder' (from *pieds poudrés*, the dusty feet of merchants who travelled from fair to fair). The great virtue of this court was its speedy action – necessary if one of the parties to a disputed bargain had to begin his journey as soon as the fair closed. And, just as many towns had more than one market, so some had more than a single fair: York, for instance, had three.

Most fairs were too large to be confined within the walls of the town and were held on the nearest convenient site outside the walls. The St Ives fair, for which the abbot of Ramsey rented out buildings, spread down the side streets and beyond the boundaries on to the open arable fields, crushing the growing crops. The fairs at Chichester and Oxford were held outside the north gate of the city. Stourbridge fair, at Cambridge, was held not in the town but at Barnwell, on the river meadows along the Cam.

To these fairs came merchants from all over Europe, as well as from all parts of Britain. To St Giles's Fair at Winchester, for example, they came from Ypres and Douai with expensive cloth, from Dinant with bronze and copper goods, from Baltic lands with wax and furs. At St Ives the booths were spread along streets arranged in 'Rows' which were named after the products traded there or the traders themselves: Lincoln, Beverley and Leicester Rows; Barkers', Spicers', Skinners', Canvas Rows – they give a good picture of the variety of trading in any fair.

King and Borough

It is now time to resume our imaginary walk through York. From the Shambles the route takes us down to Clifford's Tower – the early Norman castle. The castle as a military building will not be considered here, but its position in York serves to remind us

E

of the part the king played in town life – for originally castles in county towns were the king's and represented his authority.

York received a charter in confirmation of its privileges from Henry II, and although one-third of the 90 boroughs recorded in Domesday Book belonged to baronial lords, it was chiefly from the Crown that they obtained increasing powers of self-government. Apart from the full control of the land on which their town was built, the first of the liberties by which the burgesses set great store was the freedom to collect and pay over their own taxes to the Crown – a privilege which owed some of its importance to the fact that the sum to be collected remained fixed, even if the value of money fell. Secondly, the burgesses sought to have their own law court, in which the mayor presided. Thirdly, they aimed at full control over all local affairs, including the right to fix conditions of admission to burgess status and to appoint the members of their town council or 'corporation' – the body which by the fourteenth century was to number among its more burdensome duties the nomination of burgesses to obey the royal summons to a parliament.

In England the reigns of Richard I and John, from which about 250 borough charters survive, were a period of rapid advance, because these two kings found charter-selling was a quick way of raising money to meet their urgent needs. Thereafter, the progress of those boroughs which had no lord except the king continued rapidly. Feudal lords, such as the earls who held Leicester, Warwick, and Chester, gave way more reluctantly, and the most reluctant of all were the ecclesiastical owners of boroughs, such as the abbot of Reading and the bishop who held Wells. In Scotland the boroughs (or burghs) date only from the reign of David I (1124–53) and are predominantly of royal origin, though Dunbar was baronial, St Andrews episcopal and Canongate, the burgh of the abbot of Holyrood, lying virtually embedded in the king's capital of Edinburgh. They were later than the English boroughs in buying the right to collect their own taxes: Aberdeen was the first, settling in 1319 for £213, quickly followed by Berwick for £333 and Edinburgh for the remarkably low sum of £35 a year.

Special interest attaches to the cases where a king actually called a new town into existence and endowed it with borough status. Thus Portsmouth was created by Richard I and Liverpool by John. The best-known creations, however, are those of Edward I, designed to ensure the subjugation of Wales. Aberystwyth, Bala, Beaumaris, Bere, Caernarvon, Conway, Criccieth, Flint, Harlech and Rhuddlan are all towns of Edward's creation, though mostly based on some sort of previous settlement. The plan of these towns is of interest as revealing the mind of a medieval town-planner, even though a military one, and tends towards a symmetrical chess-board pattern. They were built quickly and labour was directed from far off to help. There were 300 labourers from Hoyland, Yorks, among the ditch-diggers at Flint and Rhuddlan in 1277 and an equal number of Derbyshire carpenters working in North Wales. All over England, masons received orders to go to Wales to work for the king; in such a way Rhuddlan, for instance, was finished in four and a half building seasons that lasted from April to November.

Edward I was also responsible for the present design of Winchelsea, an ancient associate of the Cinque Ports, where the constant erosion of the coast made it necessary to rebuild the town on a new site. This was divided into 39 'quarters', varying in size from one to three acres, through which the streets ran at right angles to each other. In these there was planned space for houses, churches and a market. The king had one English precedent to follow – a bishop who, in 1220, removed Old Sarum to grace the virgin site of the new cathedral he was about to build at Salisbury.

The Wool Trade

Let us return to York again and go down from Clifford's Tower to the waterfront, where the barges still pass by on their way down river to Hull. In the early Middle Ages, however, the Ouse connected York with places farther off – such as the Scandinavia of its early kings. The main commodity passing through York was wool, and this was by far the richest trade of the country. Eight million fleeces were exported annually in good years, partly through York and Hull but mostly through the ports of Boston, London, Southampton and Bristol. At this time not very much English cloth was exported, but the wool was eagerly sought after by the highly skilled weavers of the continent.

To such a monastery as Fountains in Yorkshire the Flemish merchant would come, riding along the rough trackways and drenched with rain across the moors. In the ample guest-house he would find shelter and plain food and men who knew him well and who would in glowing and persuasive terms speak of the wool that would fall to the shears that summer. In the days following he would ride round and handle the heavy sheep and discuss prices and delivery dates. Before he left the bargain would be struck – usually a contract for several years at a time, for nearly all monasteries sold their wool in this way and a few for as much as fifteen years ahead. Payment was often made in advance at the same time as the contract was drawn up, and in this way the merchant would obtain an easier price and the monastery, in effect, a loan on the security of its wool. As each time for delivery came round, the wool would travel by pack-horse and river down to the coast, whence the Flemings would dispatch it to Flanders in their own ships.

By the end of the thirteenth century, however, the Flemings were being ousted from the sheep farms of England by merchants from north Italy – particularly from Florence and the towns of Lombardy. The north Italian towns, unlike the Flemish, were far enough away not to be directly affected by changes in English foreign policy. The Florentines had the further advantage that their merchants were employed to collect the papal taxes in England, and it was a natural thing to transport this wealth in the form of wool. Taxes and wool, money and trade – the two went easily together, and as trading supremacy passed to the towns of north Italy, so they also became the financial hub of Europe. 'Lombard Street' was where some of these merchant financiers settled in London. Like the Flemings, the Italian merchants managed most of the wool export themselves. Their ships made some use of the eastern ports – Hull and Boston – as the Flemings had done, but they came to prefer the southern ones of London and Southampton, facing the great European overland routes to the south. This trade was a lucrative source of revenue to the English Crown, which in 1303 added a 'new custom' of 3s 4d a sack to the 'old custom' of 6s 8d.

Exports and Imports

The production of minerals was less profitable. Iron, for instance, was not much exported, though it was produced in quantity in Gloucestershire and in the Weald of Surrey and Sussex, where the artificial ponds strung like beads in the valleys reveal its early importance. These ponds were dammed up, so that a head of water was obtained which could work the bellows and hammers of the industry. At St Briavels in Gloucestershire, spades, pickaxes, horseshoes and arrows were made, but they were taken up by the royal armies and, far from there being anything left over for export, by the end of the thirteenth century iron was actually imported from Spain. Cornish tin was in demand over much of Europe, and ships from the south-west traded it to La Rochelle and Bordeaux. Derbyshire lead was exported fairly widely from Newcastle, Boston or Lynn, the demand being sustained by such orders as that for the lead roofs of the great Cistercian abbey of Clairvaux, which filled 100 carts and was conveyed by sea from Newcastle to Rouen. From Newcastle, too, there was an export of coal, amounting in good years to about 7,000 tons.

Imports, on the other hand, consisted largely of luxuries for the enjoyment of the wealthier classes, which alone had the necessary purchasing power. The finest qualities of cloth, including silk; jewels, beautifully illuminated manuscript books, and other costly rarities; and especially the spices which gave flavour to last year's salted meat – all these were in demand in castles and manor houses and, increasingly, in the homes of prosperous merchants. One bulky import was wine, the consumption of which seems to have been more widespread than in modern times. It was brought regularly from the Rhineland to Norman London, and a still bigger trade grew up a little later with Bordeaux, because Gascony became for several centuries a possession of the English Crown. As much as 4,000,000 gallons were imported in a year, mainly through Bristol, whence the barrels were distributed by road and river.

To begin with, imports as well as exports were largely controlled by foreigners and foreign shipping. Merchants from Florence,

Lucca and Siena collected papal taxes and in doing so became involved in the wool trade. Gascon ships played a large part in the wine trade with Bristol, some Gascon vintners carrying their interest in their product to the point of selling it retail in England. The north German towns of the Hanseatic League controlled the trade between England and the Baltic, and their merchants lived a separate life in the 'Steelyard' near London Bridge behind a high wall, which concealed their wharves, offices and warehouses. There, and also at Boston and Lynn, their rules kept them indoors in the evening – nor was marriage permitted between them and the English.

The ships were tiny by modern standards – even the broad-beamed 'cogs' seldom exceeded 200 tons – and this makes it easier to understand how places situated some way inland, such as York, could yet act as ports. Having steerboards rather than rudders, single, square sails, and no compass, shipping was much at the mercy of the weather and of the pirates that infested the European seas. To guard against these it became the custom, and on occasion the law, that ships sailed in convoy, thus increasing the tendency for groups of towns to act together. The English Cinque Ports – an association originally consisting of Hastings, Romney, Hythe, Dover and Sandwich – and the very powerful north German Hanseatic League illustrate this well.

Credit and Currency

Behind all this trading activity at home and abroad – the busy bargaining at market and fair, the long lines of pack-horses threading their way across country, the little ships forcing their way out of harbour to join the convoys – there was a growing need for organized money resources. It was felt at all levels, from the peasant selling his surplus for cash in the local market to the great merchant with his European commitments and to the king himself, handling the customs and fighting expensive wars. People required both a ready supply of coin and a simple credit system. It will be convenient to take the second of these first.

Money-lending for interest was forbidden by the Church, which meant that in theory only such persons as were not subject to these laws could take part in it. The Jews therefore became the main moneylenders of Europe during the early Middle Ages and groups of them were to be found in all the major towns. The interest they charged was high – on average about 40 per cent – but the risks they ran were also high. It was not easy to claim or to enforce payment from reluctant debtors, supported by the public opinion of the communities. There were frequent riots in which the Jews were the victims and the records of debts were seized and burnt, with the result that some of the earliest town houses of stone were built by Jews who wished to keep their possessions in safety. And they were taxed, and taxed again, by the kings on all sorts of occasions, such as the declaring of a war or the marriage of a royal prince. Furthermore their gains were lost at death, for the property of a Jew then fell to the king and had to be bought back by his family.

Yet in spite of all these risks, some Jews built up great wealth and were committed to large financial undertakings. Aaron of Lincoln, for example, in the twelfth century financed the building of at least nine monasteries. At about the same time there was Josce of York, one of the richest men in that city, and Aaron his son, who besides his house in Coney Street had an office in London and rode about on a beautiful black horse. In York the Jews lived among the people, scattered throughout the town, but in many places they lived together in streets known as a 'Jewry'. But the story of the Jews in England is harshly broken into in 1290, when Edward I expelled them, having taxed them into poverty and having already begun to find that the north Italian merchants could find ways to arrange loans in spite of the displeasure of the Church.

For more ordinary trade dealings, however, it was not the availability of moneylenders so much as that of ready cash that mattered. A constant supply of coinage was assisted by the decentralization of minting throughout the country. In Scotland, the right to a mint was made the basis of the burghal system in the reign of David I, who for the issue of the first Scottish coinage set up mints in Berwick, Roxburgh, Edinburgh and other burghs. At about the same period England had 30 towns with mints, ranging from London, which employed 18 minters, to some where a pair of workers could supply local needs. In the reign of Edward I England still possessed 11 mints, and at the close of the Middle Ages coins were being minted in London, York, Bristol, Norwich, Coventry, and Canterbury.

For most of the medieval period the only English coin was the thin silver penny, which bore on its obverse side the head of the king and on the reverse the name of the minter and the mint. Up to 1247, the coins bore a short cross within an inner circle and are therefore known as 'short cross pennies'. The long cross penny then succeeded these, with its cross running to the outer rim of the coin. They were thin enough to be cut along the cross into half-pennies and farthings or fourths – until Edward I introduced separate coins for small change. After short-lived attempts by earlier kings, Edward III succeeded in establishing a gold coin, the 'noble', for foreign trade, and a thicker silver coin, the fourpenny 'groat'.

The dating of coins, even to the reign of issue, is not so easy as might be thought, since the name of the king is not always accurately stated. In Stephen's reign, the civil wars between himself and Matilda made the problem of loyalty for local minters a difficult one, which was only overcome by the device of printing, instead of either name, the quite meaningless word 'Pereric'. Richard I and John, too, added to the confusion by continuing to issue coins stamped not with their own names but with that of 'Henricus' – Henry II. But the reign of Edward I was marked by an important new development, when a single Master of the Mint was appointed with responsibility for the coinage issued from all the local mints. From this time on, the names of the local minters disappear from the coinage and these craftsmen sank into oblivion – with relief, perhaps, since the customary penalty for issuing false coins was the loss of the right hand.

There were great quantities of silver pennies minted, and they were circulated throughout the country in barrels and sacks or exported in time of war to fill the royal chests. For everyone, king and merchant alike, these coins were the life-blood of all economic activity, seeping through every mercantile transaction and providing the means of, and the motive for, change in country and town alike. Without them, any developed town life and trade would have been impossible.

9

THE BUILDINGS AND WORK OF THE CHURCH

ALL over Britain today rectangles of glass and concrete rear themselves into the sky, transforming horizons that we had not
thought would change. Though the building materials in Norman
England were different, much the same was happening, and the
changes went far to underline the new world that the clash of
arms at Hastings had introduced. In all the larger towns king or
baron built stone castles and in many of them great churches were
also built, blocking the views down narrow streets and rising
above the thatched roofs of the houses. If a man had ridden from
Southampton, for instance, north towards the Scottish border
in about the year 1125, the frequent accompaniment to his journey
would have been the sounds of the sawing of timber and the
chiselling of stone. As he passed through Winchester, he would
have seen the squat tower of the cathedral already complete and
the scaffolding going up in the nave. In St Albans all the Norman
parts of the existing abbey church, including the tower, would
have been newly finished. The choir and transepts of Peterborough
would have been rising, and the centre of the west front at Lincoln
gleaming white and new on its hilltop. In York his horse's hooves
would have echoed from minster walls which had required rebuilding after the Conqueror's 'harrying of the north'. And at journey's
end, as the traveller moved towards the flashing reflections in the
bend of the Wear, he would have heard the hammering and the
shouts of men at work on the vast nave of Durham Cathedral.

The Normans were great church builders and nowhere greater
than in England. The sheer size of their buildings must have
deeply impressed men who could remember the humble scale of
even important Anglo-Saxon churches – such as the cathedral at
North Elmham in Norfolk, which was less than 140 feet long.
Only thirteen years after the Conquest they were constructing at

Winchester the squat-towered cathedral already mentioned, and giving it a length which remained unequalled in the medieval ecclesiastical architecture of western Europe. And it is not in size only that these churches impress, for the men who roofed the Durham nave with stone rather than timber were performing an engineering feat without parallel at that date except in Lombardy.

The fever of building did not touch the cathedrals alone: in towns and villages all over the country sturdy Norman churches were rising amid the clay and wattle of the lesser buildings round, their central towers buttressed on the outside and supported by massive circular pillars within. It is estimated that in Lincoln, in 1100, there were 39 churches, far more than would have been needed to contain the whole population of the town. It is evident that the place of the Church in medieval Britain was of the greatest importance.

Inside a Cathedral

The Anglo-Norman cathedrals, like those all over Europe, were built to a fairly consistent plan, which reflected the requirements of worship in the Middle Ages. This plan, in its broadest outlines, was exceedingly simple: it provided an eastern part, designed for the dramatic splendour of the Mass and containing the choir; a western part or nave, where the people worshipped; and a central crossing, separating the two and giving the whole the shape of a Christian cross. The general plan was retained even when large portions of the cathedral were rebuilt. At Canterbury, for instance, reconstruction after a fire in 1174 was the occasion for introducing the new gothic architecture from France, which soon spread to Lincoln and elsewhere. Thus Norman building, with its huge pillars and heavy semicircular arches, gave place to the so-called 'Early English' style, marked by such features as the pointed arch, the lancet window, clusters of slimmer-seeming pillars, and elaborate chiselled carvings. The 'Decorated' style, which was to follow in the reigns of the first three Edwards, explains itself – except that the elaborate stone tracery of this period provided the setting for stained glass windows which have never been equalled in later centuries.

With the exception of Salisbury (already noticed) and St Paul's, which was raised anew after the Fire of London, each of the great English cathedrals shows the labours of many generations of medieval men superimposed upon the original Norman work. They were central to the whole life of the Age of Faith: to picture what this means, it may be useful to take an imaginary walk through one of them.

The usual entrance to a cathedral for ordinary people was either at the extreme west end or on the north side of the nave. Here, nailed to the massive timbers of the door, there was in many cathedrals and in smaller churches the 'sanctuary handle' – as there is still at Durham today, held between the teeth of a grinning monster. From very early days it was accepted that a man fleeing from justice had the right to throw himself upon the mercies of God and, under certain conditions, to seek sanctuary from his pursuers within the churchyard or the church. The sanctuary handle might mark the accepted spot where such sanctuary could be claimed, the abject criminal clinging to it and submitting himself to God's judgment. But even the churchyard might give sanctuary to the man who entered it. On consecrated ground any act of vengeance took on a more heinous character: witness the horror which filled Europe in 1170 when archbishop Becket, stubborn champion of Church claims against the Crown, was murdered in his own cathedral by four knights from Henry II's court.

Inside the door of a cathedral, the great bare nave stretched away towards the darkness of the crossing and the mysteries of the altar. It would take time to get used to the dimness of the light, for in these early cathedrals the small round-headed windows, deep-set in the thickness of the walls, admitted little daylight. At first the cathedral builders would not risk the weakening of their walls – the main supports of the leaden weight of the roof – by larger windows. The word 'nave' comes from the Latin *navis*, a ship – the structure in which the people of God rode safely, as in an ark, through the floods of the world. It was the part of the cathedral where the ordinary people most often worshipped, and to its west end they came for baptism in the great leaden or stone font. The nave had no seats in those days; the people stood patiently to listen to the distant sounds from the choir or to watch processions of cathedral dignitaries make their way round the church amid the rising smoke of candles and incense. But its walls were covered with bright paintings of biblical scenes which, to people who could not read, spoke more clearly than words of the faith of the Church. At the east end of the nave, against the more westerly of the two stone screens blocking the east and west sides of the crossing, was the main nave altar where the people took Communion, probably no more often than once a year.

Outside the nave, and running along its south wall, was the cloister, a covered way surrounding a square of grass, which often linked up with the octagonal (or rectangular) building known as the chapter house. This was the meeting place for the cathedral chapter, which consisted of the main cathedral officials together with a body of about 25 priests, known as canons, whose business it was to maintain the services of the cathedral throughout the year.

Let us go back into the cathedral again and beneath the crossing and the Norman tower into the choir. Here was usually the main organ, on top of a second screen at the choir's west end – 'the pipes being all of the most fine wood and workmanshipp, very faire', as the sixteenth-century 'Rites of Durham' has it. The choristers consisted of boys and lesser clergy, while the cathedral chapter had stalls behind them on each side of the choir. These stalls had tip-up wooden seats, with a projecting ledge on the under side, so that the clergy could support themselves during the long services which required much standing. The ledges were known as 'misericords'; they often have elaborate carvings underneath, which show not only scenes from the Bible but also grotesque figures of men and animals, the latter taken from semi-mythical descriptions in popular medieval 'bestiaries' or books of beasts. Books of more practical value were those containing Church music, which were rare at first but came into increasing use after about 1100, when an accepted method of writing music came in.

The 'Chanter' sat on the north side of the choir, with the Dean's stall opposite. On the same side as the Dean but at the end nearest the altar, the bishop had his throne – the *cathedra*, from which the word 'cathedral' is taken. As the Middle Ages went on, this stall became more and more elaborate, till its pinnacles reached almost to the vaulting of the choir. Yet the bishop was not strictly a cathedral official and was not a member of the chapter; he was the ruler of the surrounding diocese.

Bishops and Church Courts

The largest of the 17 medieval dioceses was Lincoln, which was about four times its modern size, stretching from the Thames to the Humber. The job of any bishop was a varied one but, since he was a great baron as well as the ruler of a diocese, much of his time went in attendance on the king and supervision of his wide estates. In the remainder he had to carry out confirmations, ordain priests, visit and report on the monasteries within his diocese, and preside over the church courts. From the thirteenth century onwards assistant bishops, or 'suffragans', were appointed to help the bishop in these duties; he got further help from the archdeacons, who presided over some of the church courts and went round the parishes on annual inspections.

The bishop's court was housed in some part of the cathedral buildings, though it is not possible to fix it at a particular point. In Saxon times, as we have seen, the bishop sat with the sheriff in the ordinary law courts of the shire. William I, however, insisted that the Church should set up its own courts to deal with 'any matter which concerns the regimen of souls', and from this time on the bishop ceased to sit in any of the king's courts. Church law was 'canon law', which was based on Roman legal practice and differed in many ways from the legal system that was being painfully built up by the kings of England. This came to be awkward when the kings attempted to unite the country in all aspects of administration, including the legal – the more so since the church courts claimed powers over a widening list of offences and a growing number of people. The Church considered as its province all cases concerning morals, marriage and broken promises – which could be made to cover a good deal. It also claimed the exclusive right of trying any clergy, not merely priests but persons in 'minor orders', such as door-keepers, readers and servers at the altar. These wide claims came to be increasingly irksome to English kings, the more so since the penalties imposed in the church courts were often much lighter than in the king's, and it was in trying to limit their claims that Henry II quarrelled with Becket.

Quite trivial offences, such as non-attendance at church or insulting speech against the clergy, were supposed to be reported by the churchwardens, so that the records of the church courts came to immortalize such characters as 'John Johnson, a shoe-maker', who 'keepeth his bed upon the Sundays . . . as it were a hound that should keep his kennel', or 'the host of the Cock Inn', who 'says that the very sight of a clergyman makes him sick and that he is only happy when he sees a clergyman in trouble'.

Bishops were usually men of some social standing before they were elected to their office. In theory the cathedral chapter had the right to elect whom they wished, but in practice the king issued his instructions, which commonly named men within the royal circle. This was natural enough because a bishop was a chief tenant of the king, who held lands as wide as any baron and owed knight service to the king as well as his loyal counsel at the great meetings of the court. Yet, sometimes, a bishop climbed to the top from humble origins. John Pecham, archbishop of Canterbury in the reign of Edward I, came of a farming family in Sussex, and the only English pope, Adrian IV, who acceded to his throne in the same year as Henry II, was the son of a petty clerk in the employment of St Albans abbey.

Behind the high altar of a cathedral or abbey there often stood the shrine of some local saint, such as the shrine of Edward the Confessor at Westminster, of St Edmund the Martyr (a victim of the Danes) at Bury St Edmunds, of Cuthbert at Durham – though sited differently there – and, above all, of Becket at Canterbury. Such places became the focal point for pilgrimages from all over Europe and greatly enriched the fortunate owners of the shrine. The floors round the shrines became worn down by the press of countless feet, as the tales grew of miraculous cures effected by the intercession of the buried saint. Not every great church, of course, was lucky enough to be the burial place of a saint or martyr; most had to be content with more dubious relics, such as the pieces of the Cross and the hand of St James which figured among the treasures of Reading Abbey. Since it is hard nowadays to understand the importance that people in the Middle Ages attached to the physical remains of holy men, it is illuminating to read the approving account by Benedict, abbot of Peterborough, of what followed upon the murder of Becket:

> While the body still lay on the pavement, some of the towns-folk smeared their eyes with blood. Others brought bottles and carried off secretly as much of it as they could. Others cut off shreds of clothing and dipped them in the blood. At a later time no one was thought happy who had not carried off something from the precious treasure of the martyr's body.

It is against such a background that the impulse for the Crusades becomes plain – to rescue from heathen hands the greatest relic of all, the places where Christ lived and suffered as a man.

Schools and Universities

There is another part of a cathedral we should notice – the school, which was conducted under licence from the bishop. Since Latin was the language of religion as well as of all learned studies, its elements would be taught even in the humble 'song school', where young children were trained for cathedral and monastic choirs. But a cathedral had its grammar school, where boys were educated in Latin literature and composition, the art of argument, and sometimes a little law, with a view to careers in the Church. Similar schools were occasionally attached to monasteries or, more frequently, founded by lay benefactors; girls, if educated outside the home, attended a nunnery. Though the curriculum was so remote from most present-day schooling, the teacher's life was already fraught with disappointments, as the following report of an Oxford inquest shows:

> John de Neushom went after dinner to find rods for beating his pupils. He climbed up a willow to cut rods next the mill pond . . . and fell in . . . and was drowned.

The Middle Ages saw, too, the growth of universities, which

were closely connected with the Church and the study of its doctrines; the result was that throughout western Christendom
nothing was more international than learning. The first universities
arose in places where learned men settled and collected round
them students from all over Europe, which was all the easier
because Latin was the universal language of instruction. Even
before universities were formally established, there was much
coming and going among scholars of the type of the philosopher
and would-be scientist, Adelard of Bath, who soon after 1100
studied in Tours and Laon and in some of the French cathedral
schools; he also travelled through Greece, Asia Minor, Sicily, Italy
and perhaps Spain as well. Certain centres became known for
particular subjects – as, for instance, Bologna for law and Paris
for theology and philosophy – and permanent universities
developed there. It was from Paris near the end of the twelfth
century that students migrated to Oxford, whence some moved to
Cambridge in 1209 and, more temporarily, to Northampton.
In the thirteenth century three existing Oxford colleges were
founded and one at Cambridge; the first three of Scotland's four
ancient universities were fifteenth-century foundations. Meanwhile, the courses of study began to be fixed – six years for the
Master of Arts degree, to be spent in studying the so-called 'seven
liberal arts' (grammar, rhetoric, logic, arithmetic, music, geometry
and astronomy) followed by several further years for the doctorate
of divinity, civil law, or medicine.

Increase of Monasteries: The Cistercians

Half the English cathedrals were also monasteries – doing a
double job both as mother church in a diocese and as a place where
monks carried out their regular worship. A great age of monastic
development in England began with the Norman Conquest. One
of William's first acts after he became king was to found a
monastery to commemorate his victory: Battle Abbey, on the
very hill where his knights had charged against the Saxon axes.
From this time, both in town and country, the monastic walls
became a familiar feature in the medieval scene; by 1250, there
were 348 monasteries and 140 nunneries.

Not all these monasteries followed exactly the same rule of life. The ones still existing in 1066 were all of the Benedictine Order. But the most important new foundations were those of the Cistercians, whose first English monastery was built in 1118 at Waverley in Surrey, amid the sand and pine trees near Farnham. The mother house of the Order was at Cîteaux in France but, as the aim of the Cistercians was to lead a stricter life than was possible in the monasteries of the day, they looked for the most remote areas of western Europe in which to build. It was therefore in just those parts of northern England where monasteries were most rare that the Cistercians settled – in Yorkshire, for instance, at Rievaulx, Fountains, and Jervaulx. The Cistercians also settled widely in Scotland and Wales, encouraged by the favour of David I and by the friendship of the Welsh people, who had never welcomed the Benedictine monasteries, connected with the Norman kings. So there arose such daughter-houses of Cîteaux as Melrose, Newbattle and Kinloss in Scotland and Valle Crucis and Whitland in Wales.

Many people must have been attracted to the Cistercian Order by its austerity – the constant monastic silence, the infrequent meals, and the bareness of their early buildings; others found, too late, that it was too much for them. The abbot of Rievaulx heard, but probably did not heed, such complaints as this:

> Lord, my inconstancy is not equal to the burden of the Order. Everything here and in my nature are opposed to each other. . . . I am tormented and crushed down by the length of the vigils, I often succumb to the manual labour. The food cleaves to my mouth, more bitter than wormwood. The rough clothing cuts through my skin. . . . More than this, my will is always hankering after other things, it longs for the delights of the world and sighs unceasingly for its . . . pleasures.

But the Cistercian insistence on manual work was perhaps the most interesting feature of the Order. They had large estates – all the larger because they were often freed from taxes as an encouragement to cultivate the wild lands they settled in – and they cultivated them, not only by the labour of the monks themselves but also by that of lay brothers, who lived under vows and in the monastery, and were often several times as numerous as the monks. This was how the Cistercian monks came to be owners of the largest sheep runs in England and the earliest producers of English wool on a commercial basis.

Among the other more important monastic Orders in Britain were the Cluniac, with its emphasis on long and magnificent worship, the Carthusian, with its hermit monks living in almost complete isolation from each other in their cells, and that of the Augustinian (or Austin) canons, priests who worked in both cathedrals and parish churches.

The Life of a Monk

In an abbey the choir was the important part of the church, where the seven services, spread through the day and night, were sung – matins or lauds at dawn, prime at about 6 a.m., terce at 9 a.m., sext at midday, nones at 3 p.m., vespers at 6 p.m. and compline just before bed. For the night services there was a staircase leading from the monks' dormitory into the south transept, down which the shivering and yawning monks made their way into the great church with its guttering candles and monstrous shadows. In an abbey, as in a cathedral, the nave was set aside for the ordinary people, who worshipped beyond the two walls which cut it off from the choir. The Cistercians, however, living in lonely places where there were no townsmen or villagers to stand in the echoing nave, gave it over to their lay brothers.

There was not, in fact, much which distinguished an abbey from a cathedral church. Only outside the church was the difference in buildings obvious, for the abbey church was set among the living quarters of the monks. Following a fairly standard pattern, these were centred on the cloister. This was the heart of the monastery, to which only the monks could penetrate, and from it almost every part of the monastery could be reached. In its square space, dominated by the huge mass of the church and the sounds of the organ, the silence rule was absolute. On the sunnier northern side the monks often worked, looking out upon the grassy central 'garth', at desks set in alcoves called 'carrels'. At Durham they 'studied books on a desk all after noune unto evensong tyme. This was their exercise every day.' None of these carrels remain, but the alcoves they were set in can still be seen at Gloucester.

On the eastern side of the cloister was usually the chapter house, set apart for monastic business and discipline. Also on this side, but on the first floor, was the dormitory, reached by stairs from the cloister as well as by those already mentioned from the church. To this the monks retired for a short time after the main meal of the day (which came towards noon, after High Mass) and again, at about 6.30 p.m., for their much-interrupted night's sleep. Originally there were no partitions between the beds, but later cubicles were made with boarded floors and often a desk beside each monk's bed. Leading off the dormitory were the lavatories which, as at Fountains, were often drained into the stream beside which most monasteries were built. Drainage was considered important in monastic houses and was often carefully constructed in passages several feet deep and lined with stone, which have given rise to many tales of 'secret passages'.

The south side of the cloister was usually taken up with the refectory or dining-hall, under which was often a crypt for the storage of wine and beer – the usual monastic drink. The refectory was a large rectangular building, in which the main monastic officials sat at a long table, slightly raised, at one end, with the other monks at right angles to them at tables placed down the length of the hall. Here, too, silence was the rule, although during meals the monks were read to from some devotional book. Refectory roofs were more often timber-covered than stone vaulted, and it is thought that this may have been to enable the reader to be heard more plainly.

Except in Cistercian monasteries, the western side of the cloisters was usually occupied by the guest house and the lodging of the abbot. The Cistercians put their lay brothers there, with their own refectory and dormitory, separated from the monks proper. The abbot was an exceedingly important person, not only in the life of the monastery but in that of the country too. Most abbots came from aristocratic families and moved easily within the royal circle, and they were more often than not elected by the monks under pressure from the king – just as bishops were by their own chapters. This meant that they were frequently away from the monastery on affairs of state as well as on matters connected with the running of the large and scattered monastic manors. If the monastery were a Cistercian one, the abbot had to make an annual visit to Cîteaux for the yearly council of the Order. But whatever the occasion, whenever the abbot returned the monks met him in procession and conducted him to the high altar, to give thanks for his safety and receive his blessing. According to the Rule of St Benedict, the orders of the abbot were to be treated 'as if the command had come from God'; wherever he went about the monastery, the monks stood up and bowed as he passed.

Standing separate from the cloister, and usually to the east of it, were the infirmary with its own chapel and refectory and the monks' cemetery, where the monks might be required to spend some time each day in prayer for the souls of their dead brethren and in meditation upon the future state of their own. There were also numerous outhouses, covering perhaps as much as four acres.

The Friars

In the first half of the thirteenth century a new sort of monk began to appear in Britain – in some ways not a monk at all, in that his work was done not behind walls but among the people of the towns. These were the Orders of grey and black friars – the Franciscans and Dominicans. Two troubles were affecting the Church all over Europe: one was a general decline in religious devotion, reflected even in the life of the monasteries, and the other, stimulated by the growth of education, was a new desire to question the teaching of the Church. It was therefore the task of the Franciscans, followers of Francis of Assisi, to create religious warmth through their preaching, and of the Dominicans, who followed the Spaniard, Dominic, to teach in a way which would carry conviction to the intellect.

In order to reach the people, the friars settled mainly in towns, so they were less active in Scotland or Wales, where town life was little developed. Yet in Wales they were popular because they spoke to the people in their own language. Both Orders were poor by choice – not only the individual friars but the Orders themselves, which during their first period of genuine enthusiasm refused to accept any bequests. Instead, their members lived by begging and from unsolicited gifts of alms. They were also deeply attached to learning and had settlements both at Oxford and Cambridge. Among many learned friars one name must suffice: the Franciscan, John Duns Scotus, born near Roxburgh, who was one of the most influential philosophers of the middle ages – though his name comes down to us today mainly as a term of insult in the word 'dunce'.

The Parochial Clergy

Attached to the fringes of the monastic world were the 'anchorites', who dedicated their lives to God and forswore the world. They often chose to be enclosed in a cell attached to a parish church, as did St Wulfric of Haselbury in Somerset, of whom a detailed biography was written within a few years of his death in 1154. There was a constant stream of visitors to knock on the shutters of his window overlooking the churchyard, in order to gain his advice and blessing. He was on close terms with the local lord of the manor, who presented him with his own coat of mail when he complained of the excessive comfort of his hair shirt. At night he often slept by the altar steps, forsaking the wattle bed in his cell with its woven grass-rope pillow. Before the cocks crowed or the dogs began to bark from the village, St Wulfric would be awake at the altar, saying his private Mass.

But how did the ordinary parish priest live? There is no reason to suppose that the priest at Haselbury – a certain Brichtric – was other than average, so he may serve as an example. Brichtric was a married man, with a son who ran messages for St Wulfric and served at the altar. By Brichtric's time it was beginning to be accepted that no priest could make a lawful marriage, and Henry I levied fines on married priests. But the habit died hard: in Wales it was not entirely dead, even by the sixteenth century.

It is plain that Brichtric had not the education of the ruling class, for he could speak no French and could say nothing to the bishop or archdeacon when they came to the church. There was, in fact, no training or examination before a man was ordained priest, though some sort of inquiries were made about his character and health. Since most priests were men of humble – sometimes villein – families, they were probably for the most part well satisfied with the small but certain income a priest enjoyed. The main source of this was tithes – one tenth of all produce, paid by every parishioner and chiefly in kind. There were also fees from baptisms, marriages, and burials, besides the crops from a share in the open fields.

Much of the priest's time must have been spent in farming his glebe land. But looking after the church was not a mere Sunday affair: there was an early morning service of matins to be said each day, followed by Mass at 9 a.m. and vespers in the afternoon. Baptisms, however, only took place at Christmas and Whitsun and, although parishioners had to attend Mass frequently or find themselves in the Church courts, they took Communion once a year, at Easter, and probably made their confession on the same annual occasion.

As for the village church itself, it was likely to have been built by the local lord of the manor, whose descendants had the right to appoint the priest. There was no check on the number of churches that were built and, since it was a sign of status in a lord to be able to 'present' a priest to his own church, a great many more were built than were needed. And monasteries, too, became the owners of churches, receiving them and their incomes as a pious gift from lords of manors. In the thirteenth century, for instance, the four monasteries of Kelso, Paisley, Holyrood and Arbroath owned together 126 churches, and this was so common in Scotland that a system of independent parish churches never became fully developed during the middle ages.

This, then, was the Church which claimed the devotion of priest and monk, bishop and abbot and demanded the obedience of all baptized persons. At its head in England were the two archbishops of Canterbury and York. By 1203 the four Welsh bishoprics had all become subject to Canterbury. Towards the end of the fifteenth century Scotland, which had persistently refused to be subjected to York, received two archbishoprics of its own.

In practice the chief dignitaries of the Church – archbishops, bishops, and abbots – were generally chosen by the king; he needed to be assured of the loyalty of such magnates, and their offices provided a convenient way of rewarding his chief servants. In theory, however, the right of the king to make these choices was denied by the Pope, who could exercise an effective veto on the choice of archbishops at least, because each of them had to receive from him a woollen vestment known as the *pallium* before he could exercise his office. Every bishop, too, had to receive a ring and staff at the time of his elevation, and these were not in the power of the king to give, but only in that of one or other of the archbishops. On rare occasions, when the relations between king and pope were bad, the pope might be very active in forcing his choice of archbishop or bishop upon the king; but this was not the usual pattern of things. Both king and pope had an equal interest in the peace of the Church and the State it served. And the people, if their interests were to be considered, had everything to gain from such a peace.

IO

THE MAKING OF THE LAW

IN 1072 there was a dispute in the shire court of Kent between the archbishop of Canterbury and the bishop of Bayeux about the ownership of some land. To settle this, William the Conqueror personally ordered that 'there should be brought together not only all the Frenchmen in the county but also, and more especially, the English who were well acquainted with the traditional laws and customs of the land'. These 'traditional laws' were not scorned by the new wielders of power in England, who built upon existing foundations.

There were three main sorts of law court in medieval England: church courts, baronial courts, and those belonging to the king. By the time of Henry II the church courts were preventing the establishment of a single system of law throughout the country, since it was possible for such men as church door-keepers and lesson-readers, who today would not be thought of at all as clergymen, to claim 'benefit of clergy' and so be tried in the church courts with their lighter penalties. Even if only those qualified had received this benefit it would have been bad enough, but the most obvious mark of a cleric was his ability to read; a reading test therefore was thought sufficient to pick him out. A fixed passage – the so-called 'neck verse' (Psalm 51, i) – was often set, which prudent but illiterate lay criminals used to learn by heart. Benefit of clergy was thus something of a scandal, though it cannot be said that the church courts were generally bad, except in so far as they cut across the king's legal system.

The baronial courts covered a very wide field: from the ordinary manor courts on the one hand to those of the greatest barons on the other. The powers of the manor courts were limited to minor offences only: they could not touch murder, robbery and arson, for instance, and whenever the king wished he could with-

128

draw a case from the manor court to his own. However, there were a few of the greatest barons, such as the bishop of Durham and the earl of Chester, who could exercise within their courts all the authority of the king himself. As the steward of the bishop put it, 'There are two kings in England, the lord king of England and the lord bishop of Durham.'

The King's Courts

After the Norman Conquest the royal court of law at first concerned itself mainly with the offences of the great; it was a court conducted by magnates or high officials, which followed the movements of the king and the rest of his entourage. The shire court, however, continued to be what it had been in Saxon times, namely 'the great ordinary court of litigation for all the men of the shire'.[1] Under the presidency of the sheriff, it might meet as often as once a month to deal with both criminal and civil cases. The sheriffs did not act as judges, since the decisions of the court were in theory made by the qualified freeholders of the county who attended. But when important barons became sheriffs, their malpractices made it necessary for the courts to be brought more definitely under royal control, first through the replacement of over-independent sheriffs by officials of lower rank, and further by sending out royal representatives from time to time to supervise their work. Finally, the practice was adopted – occasionally by Henry I and regularly by Henry II – of sending on tour royal judges, empowered to hold on the king's behalf a special court in which trials could be conducted on the same basis as in the royal court itself. This was the origin of the modern assize courts.

Meanwhile, convenience was causing those officials of the royal court who dealt with legal matters to cease to accompany the king on his travels. Instead, their work was all done in the palace of Westminster, where Westminster Hall continued until the Victorian age to be the seat of three great courts of law. In principle, the Exchequer dealt with the royal finances, the Court of Common Pleas with disputes between subjects, and the King's

[1] F. W. Maitland: *Constitutional History of England*, p. 42.

Bench with matters involving the king. Above these there was still the king to be appealed to in his Council which, though it was not primarily a law court, dealt frequently with legal matters – particularly with appeals and petitions. Round this council, as we shall see, parliament eventually developed – and here, too, legal business was done, all the more readily because clear distinctions between judicial, legislative, and administrative business did not exist.

The Justiciar, who acted as the king's deputy when he was absent from the kingdom, perhaps visiting his duchy of Normandy, was the first head of what we might call the judicial system; he was the predecessor of the lord chancellor as well as of the lord chief justice in his dealings with the law courts. However, by about 1200 officials who discharged judicial and other duties gave place to a class of professional judges, and half a century later one of them, Henry Bracton, wrote the first great treatise 'On the Laws and Customs of England'. It is time for us, too, to turn our attention to law and custom.

The Repression of Crime

Where the criminal law was concerned, the two most difficult problems were those of catching the criminal and then of securing his conviction: the problems of police and evidence. Both of these were to some extent solved in the custom, more ancient than the Normans, of the 'hue and cry'. The thief emerging from the splintered door with his loot over his shoulder might be seen by a villager walking late down the moonlit street. It was the villager's duty, by crying 'stop thief', to bring the neighbours out to chase the criminal. If the thief were caught in this way, he might be disposed of without formal trial. The village acted as their own policemen and provided their own evidence. In the same way, the lord of the manor, catching a criminal in the very act of his crime on his own estates, might punish him without troubling to ask whether as lord of the manor he had power to deal with that offence or not. These were the ideal situations for the medieval law, where the evidence was provided by eyewitnesses and need not be seriously questioned.

Next to the eyewitness the evidence of hearsay was much valued. In small agricultural communities people knew pretty well who the criminals of the neighbourhood were and their knowledge was drawn on in the interests of justice. Twelve local men came to form a 'jury', whose job it was to 'present' to the sheriff the robbers and murderers of their locality. The shire court was not empowered to deal with such serious crimes, so the sheriff in his turn passed on the alleged criminals to the travelling judge as he came round for the assize.

In such cases the evidence of hearsay was not sufficient to condemn those presented for trial. The court looked again for the most expert eyewitness of all – the judgment of the all-seeing God. This judgment was expressed in the issue of the Ordeal, practised since early Saxon times. The accused might, for instance, be flung into a pond with his thumbs tied to his toes, the water being addressed by the priest in the following way:

> I adjure thee, O thou Water, in the name of the Father Almighty ... that thou do not in any manner receive the man N if he be guilty of that whereof he is accused, but make him swim upon thee.

If the alleged criminal floated then his guilt was proven, for the purity of the water had rejected the impurity of the man. If he sank without struggling he was held to be innocent, for the pure water received him.

It does not seem likely that such processes of law could do much to get at the truth of a case, and even in the Middle Ages some awareness of this began to dawn. It became the custom to insure against the doubtful decisions of the ordeal by banishing even the man who came out of it successfully. Thus the presenting jury's belief in his guilt had come to weigh more heavily in the balance than the result of the ordeal. When this happened, the ordeal itself could not last for long and after 1215, when priests were forbidden by the Church to take any part, it was legally abolished.

The prosecutions for crime that have been outlined here were collective ones – in effect the neighbourhood prosecuted. But individual prosecutions, either by those who had been wronged or by their relatives, were encouraged and often took place. In this

case the form of the trial was different and it reflected a struggle between two opponents, the one affirming that a wrong had been done
and the other denying it. It was in such a situation that trial by
battle was introduced by the Normans. In criminal cases the fight
was often to the death; the accused killed his challenger, or was
killed by him, or was conducted from his lost battle to the gallows.
In civil cases both sides were allowed to hire their champions. The
Scottish exchequer rolls for 1396 include a charge of £14 12s 9d
'for wood, iron, and making the enclosure for sixty persons fighting on the Inch of Perth'; one account says that there were only
seven survivors.

Little need be said about the scale of punishments applied in the
violent world of medieval England. We may remark, however, that
imprisonment featured surprisingly little within it, for, although
Henry II ordered the building of a gaol in every county town,
prisons were expensive to build and prisoners to maintain. Death,
or mutilation by the loss of a limb or blinding, were the usual
punishments for serious crimes, and much recourse was had to
fines for replenishing the exchequer. Sometimes an unsolved
murder was settled by the levying of a 'murder fine' upon a whole
village: in 1129, for instance, four Lincolnshire villages were
punished in this way. There was also banishment with confiscation
of goods.

Civil Disputes

We must now consider the civil law. In the Middle Ages it seems
from the records that this was largely concerned with land disputes.
This may have been so, but written decisions on land were so much
in demand and were so carefully preserved that their predominance
may be exaggerated. But as the Middle Ages went on, the fact that
all land was held from a lord created many complicated chains of
sub-tenancy like the following:

In Edward I's day Roger of St German holds land at Paxton
in Huntingdonshire of Robert of Bedford, who holds of Richard
of Ilchester, who holds of Alan of Chartres, who holds of
William le Boteler, who holds of Gilbert Neville, who holds

of Devorguil Balliol, who holds of the King of Scotland, who holds of the King of England.

A lord did not cease to be the lord of the land he sold – he only ceased to be the possessor. In the law courts he might still claim rights over it, rights which might be involved with other questions arising from the transfer of estates by marriage or inheritance. In a feudal society there was plenty of room for arguments about land.

At first, such arguments were commonly settled in the courts by combat, as described above. But they plainly lent themselves to more sensible methods of settlement than this, so Henry II encouraged disputants to buy writs from the royal chancery, directing the sheriffs to empanel juries of local men who knew where right lay. Procedures were arrived at for settling the most common disputes about land and a body of law was built up, which included the recognition of two principles: 'primogeniture', or the descent of both title and estate to the eldest son, and the free sale of his holding by a tenant. Each principle had important social consequences: the first ensured that the younger sons of the landed class would have to make their own way in the world, and the second that the landed class would not be confined to the families already in possession.

Common and Statute Law

The sort of law, whether criminal or civil, that has so far been considered is 'common law', not existing in a written code at all, but emerging in countless decisions from cases in the king's courts. By the end of the twelfth century these decisions, in particular those of the courts at Westminster, began to be recorded as 'precedents' on which future judgments could be based and the common law itself extended. But there was also in the Middle Ages another form of law developing, namely statute law, whose origins were mainly in parliament.

Magna Carta

The Norman kings were not great law-givers, and the laws they did give were chiefly concerned with administration. Henry II, for example, besides regulating the procedure in lawsuits about land made a famous Assize of Arms, setting out the equipment which every freeman must possess, graded according to wealth. But it was the quarrel between king John and the barons, leading to his enforced acceptance of the Great Charter at Runnymede in June 1215, that first clearly established the notion of a law which represented a carefully worked out agreement between the king and a representative body of his subjects – even though what was agreed upon was regarded as a clarification of already existing law and custom.

Most of the 61 clauses of the Charter were concerned with the feudal rights of feudal lords, but the liberties of the Church, the towns, and traders all received some protection against the king. Some of the feudal clauses, too, were capable of wider application later on. When the king was made to concede that scutages and aids were not to be levied by him without the common consent of the realm, the concession was plainly one that could some day be extended to taxation in general, giving the tax-payer the right through his representatives to determine the taxes. And in one famous clause it required only the disuse of villein-age for the Charter to be seen as the great bulwark of English liberty.

No free man may be arrested [says Clause 39] or imprisoned or dispossessed or outlawed or exiled, or in any way brought to ruin, nor will we go against him nor send others in pursuit of him, save by the legal judgment of his equals or by the law of the land.

The century which began with the baronial triumph over King John closed with the so-called 'model parliament' of Edward I, in whose reign statute law begins clearly to take shape. This was the result of a growth in the activities of the Great Council, consisting of a nucleus of the great officers of state and an outer ring of barons – the more important tenants-in-chief – whom the king had consulted at his convenience during his movements about the country and most frequently during his periods of residence at Westminster.

The Origins of Parliament

In the second half of the thirteenth century the word 'parliament' began to be used to describe some of the more important meetings of the Great Council. In such meetings there were originally no representatives of communities – the commons – but in the 1250's knights were called in to represent the shires and in 1265 representatives of the towns were brought in, too. The famous Model Parliament of 1295 was the widest extension of the Great Council ever made, since it contained the members of the King's Council together with other barons and bishops, and elected representatives of the lower clergy as well as of the shires and the towns. But in the reign of Edward I it was still exceptional for elected commoners to be called at all, and in fact they were only summoned to thirteen of the 52 sessions of his parliaments. In the fourteenth century, however, representatives of the commons began to attend parliament regularly, while the lower clergy held their meetings or Convocation elsewhere.

The town representatives disliked attending parliament, for they had to leave their homes to travel to Westminster and stand in tongue-tied silence among their social betters. Even the knights of the shire looked down on the burgesses, because they themselves were all landholders and men of some standing in their counties. But both groups no doubt were glad when the elected commons began to meet separately from the rest of parliament, in surroundings where they could speak their minds freely and not be overawed by their greater colleagues. By the close of the fourteenth century they were sitting in the chapter house of the abbey of Westminster, at times when the monks did not use it: this was the first House of Commons chamber.

It has already been remarked that there were 52 sessions of parliament held, at irregular intervals, in the 35 years of the reign of Edward I. In the earliest days they had no fixed place – just as the meetings of the Great Council were located in accordance with the movements of the king and his court about the country. In the fourteenth century, however, the meetings of the Great Council and therefore of parliament were confined to Westminster, so that by this time the whole of the central government was carried on round the king's palace above the marshes of the river.

The expansion of the Great Council into a parliament is closely related to the increase in the wealth of the country at this time.

Plate 18. *Chapel of St John in the Tower of London.* About 1080 – a superb example of an early Norman church, with a very rare stone tunnel-vault and massive pillars, whose capitals bear a T-shaped decoration confined to this early period. In general, however, it is austerely plain; and this, too, argues a date not far removed from the first years of Norman rule. (Cf. text pp. 113–14.)

Plate 19. *Misericord (Chichester Cathedral).* Fourteenth century. This is number 16 on the south side of the choir, going from east to west – and shows two seated musicians playing a harp and recorder. (Cf. text p. 116.)

Plate 20. *The Martyrdom of St Thomas Becket.* From an English psalter of about 1200. It shows the changes that had taken place in armour since Hastings: the flat-topped helmet (not yet covering the face completely, as it did later), the hauberk extended to give protection to the hands and forearms, and the provision of mail coverings for the legs. The swords are much like those at Hastings, as are the shields, though perhaps they have shortened a little – they were shorter later – and one already displays heraldic decoration. But the time is clearly transitional, and neither knight has fully adopted the new trends. (Cf. text pp. 146–7.)

Plate 21. *The clash of battle.* This shows very well the armour of the first half of the 13th century. Headgear varies from the closed 'helm' with eye-slits to the open-front 'coif' (usually part of the mail hauberk) and the broad-brimmed 'kettle hat', worn especially by common soldiers. The hauberk extends from the head to hands and feet (which are equipped with 'prick' spurs) and is covered by a loose 'surcoat' – already, like the shields and pennants, carrying heraldic design. Surcoats (in one case heraldic) are also worn by the horses, whose high-backed saddles gave support in war and jousting. (Cf. text pp. 146–7.)

Plate 22. *The Tower of London.* Nicolaus Pevsner calls this 'the most important work of military architecture in England' (*Buildings of England* series – London I, p. 184). It certainly shows very clearly the medieval developments of castle-building: from the square Norman keep in the centre (completed in 1097 and called 'white' because originally whitewashed) to the two outer rings of curtain walls punctuated by towers, so typical of the 'concentric' form of castle. These walls are 13th century – the inner, and part of the outer, built by Henry III and the remainder by Edward I. (Cf. text p. 151.)

Plate 23. *Ploughing.* From the 14th-century Luttrell Psalter. The mechanical details of the plough can be seen: the coulter making the first cut into the soil, the beaked ploughshare penetrating it more deeply, and the mould-board turning it over. The mallet was used to bang down the coulter and ploughshare to give a deeper cut. (Cf. text p. 89.)

Plate 24. *A cart with dogs.* From an early 14th-century edition (in the British Museum) of the Raymond of Penafort compilation of the Decretals of Gregory IX – written in Italy but illustrated in England. Dogs were not often used as draught animals in the Middle Ages, but this is only a light cart. These dogs are probably mastiffs, though villeins were not encouraged to own large dogs because of the likelihood of poaching (see page 82).

Plate 18

Plate 19

Plate 20

Plate 21

Plate 22

tue letificauerunt animam meam.

Numquid adheret tibi sedes iniqui
tatis: qui fingis laborem in precepto.

Captabunt in animam iusti: +san
guinem innocentem condempnabunt.

Plate 23

Plate 24

Royal taxation had to tap this, in order to meet the growing expenses of the king in Scottish and Welsh wars and in the defence of the English possessions in France. The obligation that rested upon a feudal lord to seek the consent of his chief tenants when he intended raising a money 'aid' from them was one reason why the king summoned his Great Council to meet him at regular intervals. It had become an accepted idea that men should be consulted before they were taxed, and it was natural therefore for such kings as Edward I to seek agreement to taxation from the commoners who now represented the growing wealth of the country.

But there is another aspect of parliament which it is important to note in these early stages – the legal one. This is most clearly seen if one looks at the nucleus of the thirteenth-century parliament in the king's own court, which was not just a ceremonial affair but was in fact a law court too, to which appeals and petitions had always been directed. This remained true as the king's court, where his personal advisers were to be found, was widened into the Great Council and then again into parliament. Parliament is still the 'High Court of Parliament', and the House of Lords still a final court of appeal. With the king's approval, parliament from an early date heard petitions which were often legal in character. These came up from men who had received no satisfaction in a lower court, or who had suffered wrongs that such a court was unable to deal with. In considering these matters parliament was acting in a legal capacity, but it was also in process of producing a new sort of law. A petition to parliament often had an application and an importance much wider than the interests of the person who presented it. Parliament's decision in such a case therefore had the effect of laying down the law for everyone.

This sort of general legal decision came to be known as a statute and was the foundation of statute law. Not everything that parliament dealt with in this way, however, originated as a petition. Sometimes the king would bring before it general matters other than taxation, for which he wanted its support; what parliament agreed to in these matters likewise became part of statute law. Edward I's great statutes concerning land ownership, commerce, and police represent to some extent the agreement of his

F

parliaments, even if it was often in the form of the silence that gives consent.

Nevertheless, our natural interest in the evolution of parliament must not be allowed to obscure the fact that Edward I was viewed by contemporaries as pre-eminently a law-giver, witness the following passage from a chronicle kept by a monk at Norwich for the year 1285:

> King Edward reached London on his return after Easter from the subjugation of Wales . . . and went in solemn procession on foot from the Tower of London to Westminster, with Queen Eleanor, all the magnates of the realm and fourteen bishops. John Pecham, the archbishop of Canterbury, carried the cross which the king had captured in Wales. On that day the king opened his parliament at Westminster; it lasted seven weeks and in it the king established very many new laws, knighted very many sons of magnates and confirmed many charters of his ancestors who were kings of England.

Legal Institutions of Scotland and Wales

Finally, a brief comparison of the legal systems in Scotland and Wales. In the thirteenth century the Scottish kingdom moved a further long step towards unity, when first the mainland counties in the far north, and then the Hebrides and Isle of Man, were wrested from the Crown of Norway, leaving only the Shetlands and Orkneys to be added at the very close of the Middle Ages. Even so, Scottish law originates in four separate sources – Roman, canon, feudal and English law – and it is perhaps surprising that Celtic law does not also figure among them. But in Scotland, as in Wales, Celtic law was tribal and family in character and was not readily applicable to national needs. David I, who by marriage was earl of Huntingdon in England, where he had also spent much of his youth, knew a good deal both of feudal law and of Anglo-Norman statecraft, so that in his reign Scotland was deeply affected by feudal and English law. Yet the influence of the Church was also strongly felt, especially through the activities of judges-delegate appointed by the Pope. Scotsmen were more free to choose the processes of the church courts than the English were, since the centralization of the king's courts had not gone so far. For the same reason large and small baronial courts flourished with less hindrance than in England.

The pattern of the king's courts was very similar to the English – with the King's Council at the head of the pyramid, travelling about with the king and doing justice. Sometimes the king himself settled cases – as was reported by Ailred of Rievaulx in the reign of David I:

> It was his custom to sit at the entrance to the royal hall and carefully hear the cases of poor men and old women who were called to him individually in whatever district he came to, and to satisfy each, often after much deliberation.

David I took the idea of the sheriff from England and set up 'sheriff courts' throughout the country, whose function was rather like that of the English shire court. By the thirteenth century Scotland also had royal judges who went on tour within their districts, whether Galloway, Lothian or 'Scotia' (north of the Forth).

The Scottish parliament came into existence at about the same time and in much the same way as the English. It arose out of meetings of the king with his Council, to which the name of parliament was first applied in 1293; three years later Edward I of England received the (temporary) submission of the northern kingdom from a parliament of two thousand Scots at Berwick. The calling of town representatives or burgesses to parliament is first mentioned in 1326 and then again, more clearly, in 1357. The general reason for it was the same as in England – the expense of war; in 1357 there was also a special reason, namely the need to raise a huge ransom for David II, who had been for eleven years a captive of the English Crown.

In Wales the development of the law was not proceeding in the same direction as in the two neighbouring countries. In a country as divided as Wales, with English Marcher earls occupying the south and threatening the north and with the people themselves in many respects disunited, the firm establishment of a nation-wide legal system was a luxury that had to await more settled times. Such times did not come until after the Principality had lost its freedom.

The basis of Welsh law was the family and the tribe rather than the nation. It was codified by Howell the Good in the tenth century, but three hundred years later there was a period of considerable revision and modernization. In both criminal and civil law, however, the basic unit was still the kindred, which was wide enough to include fifth-cousins and which possessed rights of land ownership. Blood feuds and the payment of wergild also survived much longer in Wales than in England.

The most important Welsh court was that of the 'commote', which was an administrative area rather like the English 'hundred', based on kindred groups. But Llywelyn the Great and his grandson of the same name, who in 1267 was acknowledged as prince of Wales, set up a High Court to hear appeals from the commotes and to settle disputes between the Welsh princes. Indeed, this institution was rather more than a court, for it was used by the prince for consultation in government and was roughly representative of the princely family, the leading clergy, and the minor lords, at least of North Wales, on which his power was centred.

However, the completion of the conquest of Wales by Edward I turned the development of Welsh law into other courses and, as far as the criminal law was concerned, assimilated it to English legal practice. The newly annexed parts were divided up into five shires, and shire courts and sheriffs were introduced. In theory, Welsh civil law remained intact, and Welsh local officials continued to work under the sheriffs. But as the Welsh were actively encouraged to adopt English law instead, it took only about a century for Welsh civil law also to fall into disuse, except (surprisingly enough) in some of the Marcher lordships and as regards the continuing preference for inheritance by the kindred rather than primogeniture.

In all parts of the island, then, these centuries were in one way or another a great period in the making of law and in the development of representative institutions. These were the peaceful landmarks of the age: we must notice next its military characteristics.

THE LATER MIDDLE AGES

II

WARS AND WARFARE

WAR played a considerable part in the life of England under her Norman kings. Besides the baronial wars already mentioned, she was involved in those which arose out of the continental ties of her sovereigns, such as that in which John lost Normandy. But from the reign of Edward I (1272–1307) onwards, the influence of war seems more pervasive.

He crowned the long-drawn-out advance of the border barons into Wales in two campaigns of conquest, using a fleet from the Cinque Ports so as to attack Snowdonia from Anglesey. Although two revolts had to be suppressed in the later years of the reign, Welsh independence came to an end with the surrender of Bere castle, near Cader Idris, in April 1283. Thereafter the building of royal castles and boroughs enforced a new order upon an unhappy but powerless people.

Edward I also claimed sovereignty over Scotland. Taking advantage of a disputed succession – in 1291 there were thirteen claimants to the throne – he overran the country with his troops both before and after a nationalist rising under William Wallace, who was defeated at Falkirk in 1298. In September 1305 Edward issued his Ordinance for the Government of Scotland, recently described by a Scottish historian as 'a statesmanlike document';[1] but when he died the national cause was still maintained in arms by a rival king, Robert Bruce, who had been crowned at Scone

[1] W. C. Dickinson: *Scotland from the Earliest Times to 1603,* p. 161

the previous year. Bruce's overwhelming victory at Bannockburn (1314) over Edward II, a weak successor who was eventually deposed, undid the work of his mighty father, and although English arms were again successful at Halidon Hill and Northallerton, Scottish independence was safeguarded by the 'auld alliance' with England's enemies in France.

The Anglo-French struggle known as the Hundred Years War, which was fought intermittently from 1337 to 1453, had no better cause than Edward III's warlike ambitions, but it is impossible to deny the importance of its military events, brilliantly described – as far as the year 1400 – in the chronicle of the Fleming, Jean Froissart. Famous victories won by the king himself at Crécy and by his son, the Black Prince, at Poitiers marked the first phase of the struggle; but in the last years of Edward's reign and in that of his young grandson, Richard II, England lost most of her gains in France. In 1415, however, Henry V's triumph at Agincourt brought English fortunes to their zenith: in 1431 his infant son and successor, Henry VI, was crowned King of France in Paris. Yet by that time the revival of the French national spirit had been begun by Joan of Arc, and when the final peace was made in 1453, England retained only Calais. The returning troops then provided the manpower for the brutal domestic conflicts, afterwards dignified with the name of The Wars of the Roses.[1]

This bare outline of events is perhaps sufficient to justify consideration at this point of the general character of the warfare in which the British peoples were so frequently engaged.

The Military Life

For most people, whether enforced combatants or passive victims, war was a harsh interruption of their everyday lives. But for king, baron, or knight it might wear a different aspect. 'Prowess,' declared Froissart, 'is the mother stuff and the light of noble men and, as the log cannot spring to life without fire, so the noble man cannot come to perfect honour or to the glory of the world without prowess.' Hence the prominence in the records of this period of the tournament, which a contemporary writer

[1] See p. 194

defines as a military exercise carried out, not in the spirit of hostility but solely for practice and the display of prowess.

At the outset the tournament had not been very different from a battle engagement: groups of armed horsemen took sides and charged each other with catastrophic consequences. In 1179 the Church forbade Christian burial to the slain, which may have resulted in more vigilant efforts to enforce rules requiring the use of blunted weapons. But it is likely that the main ameliorating influence was that of kings, who feared a disastrous breach of the peace. Henry II forbade tournaments outright. Edward I allowed only a less murderous type of encounter between individuals, called a joust; there was large-scale jousting in 1284 to celebrate the conquest of Wales. Finally, in the fifteenth century a stout barrier or 'tilt' was laid the length of the jousting field, so that the blunted lances of the combatants, and not their horses and persons, met in the headlong charge. Once recovered from their sprains and slipped discs, knights who kept in training in this fashion would be ready to campaign in earnest, sharing Froissart's enthusiasm for 'the fresh shining armour, the banners waving in the wind, the companies in good order riding a soft pace.'

A more material aim for most men who took part in war was the chance of plunder, and this involved poor and rich alike. Whether staggering through the fires of a burning village with bales of cloth or lying by the roadside befuddled with French wine, there were times when a medieval soldier found war to have compensations. The richest of all was the chance of ransom – the best sort of plunder that war provided. This could do much to moderate the slaughter of battle, as a certain John Jewel appreciated who, in 1364, had his helmet engraved with the information that 'whoever captures John shall have 100,000 francs'. The bigger the catch, the bigger the prize and to some extent the same was true of the captor: a man of position could demand a higher ransom than the lower ranks. Still, even unimportant people could find profit in ransoms, as did John Ballard, an archer at Crécy who, having captured the archdeacon of Paris, deserted from the army and made his way to London, where he sold his prize for £50. And there was John Coupland, who did even better for himself at the battle of Neville's Cross near Durham in 1346.

At the price of two teeth left upon the battlefield, he captured David II of Scotland, delivered him to Edward III, and won £500 a year for life. But earlier than this the Scots, too, had been glutted with so much plunder and ransom from English barons after Bannockburn that it was said, 'Scotland became rich in one day'.

Military Organization

But the wars for which the trumpet sounded in the Middle Ages had many sterner aspects. It is therefore reasonable to ask, as men rode or marched in to answer the call, what the king's claim to their duty was.

In the early Middle Ages men were mustered for war through two main obligations – either the feudal duty of serving the king as lord in return for lands held from him, bringing mounted knights for service in number proportionate to the size of holding; or the general duty, descending from the old Saxon fyrd, that required all able-bodied men to serve the king if called on.[1] The former provided the aristocratic mounted element in the army and the latter the ordinary foot-soldiers. The army of landholders – the feudal army – by itself provided the Norman kings with a force of about 6,000 men, to which the old fyrd, now known as 'shire-levies', could add many thousands more, county by county.

But, as the Middle Ages went on, kings found it increasingly difficult to raise the numbers that the feudal armies had once provided – and hard, too, to keep them together for long. When the first generation of military barons died they left their lands, and with them their obligations as warriors, to their sons; and the knights under these barons, landholders themselves by favour of their lords, did the same with their own lands and duties. But there could be no certainty that these sons – and grandsons – would take easily to a life of arms. Moreover, a single knight's holding of land might be divided among several heirs, with the result that someone could find himself bound to provide the king with a half or a quarter of a knight! The expense of keeping ready for war, too, constantly went up, both in armour and horses.

[1] See pp. 60 and 67

Furthermore, the feudal army had an obligation to serve its lord free of charge for at most two months in the year, and there were few campaigns of importance that could be finished in this time – especially those in France. In fact, there was an under-standing that no feudal army should be required to serve overseas; in 1205 an expedition sent by John to try and recapture Normandy had actually to be cancelled because the troops refused to sail.

In these circumstances the numbers of men available through the feudal summons to landholders greatly declined, and it is not surprising that kings from Henry I on should have tried to gain a more reliable turn-out by demanding money rather than knights from their tenants and using this to hire either native troops or foreign mercenaries. Henry I began the practice with some of his Church barons, bishops and abbots, who often failed to produce efficient knights anyway. They paid a tax, 'scutage' or shield-tax, at the rate of eightpence a day for each knight that they should have produced. Later the tax was allowed, as an alternative to providing knights, to other than Church lords. And King John went so far as to grant new land to his barons, not for military service but for cash.

With money gained in this way – and by general taxation as well – medieval English kings were able to hire Welsh infantry (especially archers) and some mercenaries from central Europe, as well as pikemen from Brabant and Genoese crossbow-men. Soon the shire-levies themselves were paid, at least for any long period of service; and the payment of native soldiers became more usual after Magna Carta tried to stop the employment of foreign mercenaries.

In the later thirteenth century a new device for recruitment was gaining ground – that of contract. A lesser baron who made war a profession would make an agreement with the king to supply him with any men he needed – mounted men-at-arms, spearmen and archers: in the end, even chaplains and surgeons. Rates of pay and length of service were decided and contracts eventually drawn up in duplicate, the king keeping one copy and the con-tractor the other. By the time of Edward III the whole army was paid – even the Black Prince taking £1 a day.

The feudal army, in fact, disappears so completely by the

fourteenth century that we learn with surprise of the continuance of the conscript shire-levies, even though they too became paid men. Archers in Edward III's reign, for instance, received 6d a day. But the shire-levies were much too useful to be abandoned: they could be employed to garrison or besiege castles and for all sorts of rough jobs, such as building the roads that Edward I required in north Wales. But more than anything else they were vital in defending the north against Scottish invasion, as the Yorkshire levies had done in 1138 at the Battle of the Standard.

Arms and Armour

'Our heads are covered with helmets', said a Scottish bishop before the battle in 1138, 'our breasts with coats of mail, our thighs with greaves, and the whole of our bodies with shields. Wherever the enemy strikes, he will not find one unprotected by iron.' This description corresponds fairly closely with what Henry II's Assize of Arms ruled as necessary for a knight: hauberk, helmet, shield and lance. The hauberk was a shirt of chainmail reaching to the elbows and thighs. By the thirteenth century the mail covered the whole body, extending both as stockings from the hips down and as long mittens on the forearms, with holes in the palms so that the hands could be kept free. Beneath the hauberk there was a 'gambeson' – a leather garment quilted with a cross-stitched cover of cloth or silk. With such a backing the hauberk could not be pierced by a lance nor slashed by a sword, and was all the stronger when it was extended from the neck to cover the whole head except the face, removing the necessity for a helmet save to guard against a hard bang. The helmet had changed a good deal from the conical protection with its nose-piece that the Bayeux Tapestry shows: this nose-piece could be seized and the helmet's wearer made helpless. The helmet was now extended to cover the face completely, with the exception of slits for the eyes and holes for breathing. At the same time the conical top was flattened, so that it looked like an upturned saucepan. This shape did not deflect blows, as the conical helmet had done; it could also be knocked sideways, so that nothing could be seen from the eye-slits, or it could be dented. Once when a certain battered knight was the winner in a tournament, he was presented with his prize in a smithy, where he lay with his head on the anvil getting the dents knocked out of his helmet so that he could take it off!

The protection afforded by the knight's armour increased between the eleventh century and the thirteenth, when plate-armour began to appear. Chainmail had never protected very well certain parts of the body, such as knees, armpits and shoulders, and plate was at first strapped on as isolated protection for these places. Eventually, however, full suits of plate armour were introduced, which made shields almost superfluous. They consequently became a mere background for heraldic decoration, the coat of arms by which the warrior, now completely encased in armour, could be identified. Even at Hastings William himself was only recognizable when he raised his helmet. Such decoration was later also applied to the 'surcoat', which in the thirteenth century was worn over the armour as a sort of light overall to protect it from rain and rust. As for the knight's weapons, the Assize of Arms mentions a lance – a sort of spear, often with a fluttering pennant attached – and the long sword reaching as high as a man's waist is familiar from crusaders' effigies.

All this concerns the upper classes. The Assize of Arms, however, also took into account ordinary freemen. They were to have at least a gambeson, an iron cap of sorts, and a lance. This lance varied from a simple spear to a bill, which could both cut and thrust and even pull down horsemen with its hooked blade. By the thirteenth century, ordinary foot soldiers had also to possess bows and arrows.

There had been bows at Hastings – short light ones, whose strings were drawn back only to the chest and whose arrows could not penetrate deeply. But in the twelfth century they were supplemented by the crossbow – a much more powerful affair, with its wooden stock supporting a metal bow and string. This had to be pulled, or even winched, back before being triggered off to impel a metal bolt along a groove in the stock and so into the air. But such a bow was too expensive to be used widely by conscript armies and needed skilled strength to work it well. It became the speciality of mercenary soldiers such as the Genoese, whose archers were employed by many medieval kings.

The longbow originated in south Wales in the later twelfth century, and was brought into use against the armies of the Marcher lords and Edward I's expeditions of conquest. At Falkirk it was employed against the Scots by Welsh archers in Edward's pay, but it was not fully developed until the Hundred Years War. The longbow had a six-foot span and fired an arrow a yard long. It was made of tough woods, such as yew, and was drawn to the ear rather than the chest, the archer standing sideways to his target to do so. The combination of the toughness of the wood with the tension of the fully drawn string gave remarkable penetrating power: the arrow would pierce chainmail at 250 yards as a normal range. The longbow was lighter than a crossbow and could be fired more quickly – ten or even twelve arrows a minute as compared with two crossbow bolts. But its effective use required a long-continued development of strength and skill. The story of victories won with the 'grey goose-feather' created a national tradition, so that successive generations of boys practised eagerly at the butts with bows scaled down to match their age.

Battle Tactics

There were very few large set battles fought by the new rulers of England in the period after Hastings, because for most of the time defence was stronger than attack and wars tended to peter out in fruitless sieges of castles. Thus the long internal struggle of Stephen's reign produced only two battles, and neither Henry II nor Richard I fought a single large-scale engagement in their wars in France. Much fighting went on in Wales, but even in the time of Edward I no great battles took place, for the mountains made the movement of large invading armies and their transport difficult, while the Celtic temperament preferred to base resistance upon dashing individual raids rather than long, doggedly-fought battles. But the Anglo-Scottish duel, with its four big battles in half a century, and the principal campaigns of the Hundred Years War were fought differently. The fact that they did not become bogged down all the time before increasingly elaborate castles is due mainly, perhaps, to the growth of nationalism. The Scots and French, to say nothing of the English, were feeling their way towards a sense of national separateness; wars therefore became inspired with a new fury, which could not find its satisfaction in the slow reduction of fortified places.

At Hastings the Normans had launched mounted charges against the Saxon foot, and the weight of such charges was to be a main feature of open battles for three or four centuries. An armoured knight made a very formidable impact, if the going on the battlefield was good and his horse fresh; it was common for an esquire to hold one or two extra chargers (worth £100 apiece) in reserve. Yet most of the decisive fighting was done on foot, often by dismounted knights laying about them with their swords.

The chief Scottish weapon was the 18-foot pike, wielded to deadly effect by 'round battles' or *schiltroms* of foot: these were tightly packed oblong formations, in which the front rank knelt with their spear butts on the ground, while those in the rear stood up with their spears levelled over the heads of their fellows. At Bannockburn, where the English archers were misplaced and were ridden into the mud by light horsemen, the schiltroms largely won the day. But the English soon learnt to use the longbow defensively, employing for the first time at Halidon Hill in 1333 the tactics which were to secure their great victories in France.

The archers were placed on the flanks of the divisions of dismounted spearmen and at a wide angle to them, so that they enclosed the enemy cavalry charge and held it beneath a shower of arrows from two sides. Various devices were tried to ensure that hostile cavalry should not ride down the archers – from mingling spearmen with them to digging holes or planting sharpened stakes on their front. For to stand up to a cavalry charge must have been a testing experience, even for these archers, many of whom themselves normally operated as mounted men. On the field of battle, however, their horses were confined with those of other mounted infantry in the baggage train, ready, at least in theory, for the pursuit.

Transport and Supply

How were these armies supplied? It was never an easy matter to feed and clothe an army on the march and in winter it was almost impossible, for wagons had to keep to the roads even in the best of times and in the worst they were stuck. In summer the problem was eased, though not solved, by living off the land, though this obviously antagonized the people of the countryside. Stripped fruit trees (and the six-foot bill-hook was ideal here) together with empty barns and cowsheds marked the passage even of friendly armies, while hostile ones looted farm-houses and left them burning. Bread was the usual food of the troops, supplemented rarely by meat. As far as possible it was baked during halts between marches, and any cattle that had been rounded up were then slaughtered. But supplies were also bought along the line of march, no doubt at low prices which civilians dared not refuse.

Much of these provisions had to accompany the army and its munitions of war, so there was a further problem of finding enough wagons and horses or oxen. Scottish armies usually travelled light: in the words of Froissart, they 'bring no carriages with them on account of the mountains they have to pass'. The sturdy ponies, on which they were accustomed to sweep across the Border, sufficed for their simple needs.

Neither do they carry with them any provisions of bread or wine, for they will live for a long time on flesh half-sodden, without bread, and drink the river water. They have therefore no occasion for pots or pans. Under the flaps of his saddle, each man carries a broad plate of metal; behind the saddle a little bag of oatmeal; when they have eaten too much of the sodden flesh, and their stomachs appear weak and empty, they place this plate over the fire, mix with water their oatmeal, and when the plate is heated, they put a little of the paste upon it and make a thin cake, like a biscuit, which they eat to warm their stomachs.

With the English army things were very different: when Edward III's troops left Calais in 1359, six thousand wagons rumbled out of the town. Like the supplies they carried, many of these wagons had been forced into service at the king's command and not always even at a price. There can have been little joy at the approach of even the friendliest army and few genuine smiles of welcome.

Edwardian Castles

Meanwhile, the relatively simple form of castle, which had done so much to make warfare static in the early Norman period, was beginning to be menaced by advances in siege methods. As the power of the besiegers increased, it became necessary to push them farther away from the heart of the castle. A new pattern of castle was therefore quickly developed, starting with those built in the Levant by the Crusaders and reaching its peak of splendour in Britain with the Welsh castles of Edward I. These castles are concentric – that is, they consist of an inner heart (the old keep) surrounded by one or more outer 'curtain' walls, usually at a lower level. Rectangular towers gave way to round ones, not only at the centre but also at frequent intervals along the curtain walls. This was done, for example, at the Tower of London, where twelve such towers were constructed in the inner ring of wall surrounding the White Tower, chiefly under Henry III.

These round towers projecting from straight wall surfaces were a valuable military acquisition, enabling the whole wall area between one tower and the next to be covered by fire from each side as well as from the battlements above. The towers also formed strong-points in the defence of the castle, which could be contested one by one if the wall itself was somehow breached.

Edward I employed an Italian castle-builder of genius, James of St George, who became 'Master of the king's works in Wales'. Between 1277 and 1301, while the country was being subjugated, eight castles were built with the help of enforced labour from all over England. These were Flint, Rhuddlan, Builth and Aberystwyth, followed by Conway, Harlech and Caernarvon, and finally Beaumaris. All these are roughly concentric, but with great variations in detail – for it would have been foolish and wasteful to have applied the pattern rigidly on sites, such as that of Flint on the river Dee, where natural defences made artificial ones less important. The most vulnerable point was always the gatehouse, which was therefore given the most elaborate protection. At Caernarvon, in order to reach the inner bailey from the King's Gate, it was necessary to cross the drawbridge, to pass through five doors and beneath six portcullises, and then to make a right-angle turn from the main to a smaller passage leading to a second drawbridge at the end. The whole route was also furnished with arrow-slits and holes in the vaulting, through which further attentions could be showered upon unwanted visitors.

The towers and dungeons of these vast structures provided plenty of space to stock food and munitions. When Edward I's Scottish headquarters were at Berwick castle in 1298, the carefully listed stores included even such items as the following:

Two light hauberks without hoods, three hauberks of strong iron without hoods, five pair of covertures of iron and two headpieces of iron, two pairs of shoes of iron, six old targes, one old shield, one targe of boiled leather, one pair of firepans, four boxes, seven crossbows with winches with old cords, and four of them are out of order for want of cords, six crossbows for two feet, one of which wants two cords and one nut . . . eight crossbows for one foot, all in order excepting four nuts, one 'teller' with a winch, and one for one foot, four old bands, one coffer, three vices, one quarter of canvas, 189 wings of geese for feathering crossbow bolts.

To starve a garrison into surrender was therefore a long and costly business. Down to the reign of Henry V, when a siege-train of primitive guns came into play for bombarding fortresses, direct attack was also very difficult, but it had often to be attempted.

Siege Methods

For battering castle walls and destroying their defenders, it was usual to employ a variety of siege machines, worked by torsion, tension, or counterpoise. The 'mangon' and the 'trebuchet' both lobbed heavy stones at or over the castle wall, while the 'arbalest', a kind of mammoth crossbow, projected iron bolts. Burning material, too, was hurled in to set fire to roofs and wooden outbuildings.

Sometimes the walls were climbed, either by means of scaling-ladders with hooked upper ends that gripped the castle parapet, or with the expensive but formidable siege tower, such as the Crusaders had used in 1099 at the capture of Jerusalem. This was a tower built up storey by storey until it was higher than the wall. Then it was moved forward on rollers across the laboriously filled-in moat until the wall itself came within reach of a projecting platform on top.

However, unless a castle was built on solid rock or completely surrounded by deep water, the most hopeful method of attack was likely to be mining. A tunnel was begun at a safe distance from the fortress, preferably by experienced men (such as the miners of the Forest of Dean) who knew how to shore up their work properly as they went along. When the sappers had reached the base of the castle-wall, they dug out as many as possible of the great stones and replaced them by temporary supports of timber, packed round with straw and brushwood. The garrison were then invited to surrender, and if they refused the mine was fired, the wall was breached, and the besiegers charged yelling through the gap. Disastrous hitches often intervened, but this is roughly how king John's men, for example, broke into the castle at Rochester, where the marks of the subsequent repairs can still be seen on one of the corners of the great tower.

In such ways as these did men prepare for wars and fight them in medieval Britain, whether tramping across country with coloured banners glinting in the sun or splashing miserably through drenching rain, whether looking down hungrily from castle walls or looking warily up at them to place a scaling-ladder. In any case the soldier was generally a countryman and would take the first opportunity to return to his fields – where we may now follow him.

12

THE CHANGING VILLAGE

FOR many generations the agricultural routine, as established in England by the Saxons, continued with very little change in virtually self-sufficient village communities. A good harvest meant full stomachs, a poor one was followed by a winter of near-starvation. But whatever the results, for the most part men still laboured at the earth in the way their forgotten ancestors had done, until they too were buried in it at last.

In the twelfth and thirteenth centuries, however, various modifications were gradually introduced to meet new needs. The tiny population of medieval England had at last begun to rise more rapidly: in 1300 it may have been approaching three and a half millions. This created a demand for additional crops, to be grown on new land or by more intensive cultivation of the old. The monks of Christ Church, Canterbury, began to drain Romney marsh, a start was made on enclosing the fens on the edge of the Wash, and all over the country new intakes encroached upon woodland and waste. Marling (the Roman practice of treating light soils with limy clay, so that they held moisture) was reintroduced, and in some places a two-field was altered to a three-field rotation, so as to reduce the amount of temporary fallow by one-sixth. New villages sprang up – many on the border of Wales, for instance – though not all were of the compact type familiar in the midlands and south of England. Altogether, the number of villages was greater than in the vastly more populous England of today.

New opportunities of profit were seized upon by owners of big estates, both lay and ecclesiastical, who did everything they could to make the cultivation of the demesne lands efficient. Large crops of corn (and wool) were sent even to distant markets, conveyed there by grumbling villeins. From the Huntingdonshire abbey of

Ramsey, for example, they had sometimes to cart for their lords as far as Colchester, London, or Canterbury. Villeins also learnt to market their own surplus harvest, at least in the nearest town. By the thirteenth century, treatises on farming enabled rather better methods to be adopted by anyone on the land who could read, which meant chiefly the monastic landlords; but the most striking changes were still in matters of organization.

Commutation of Labour Services

Perhaps the manor, even in midland England, had never been so clearly divided between free and unfree – the lord and his free tenants on the one hand, the villeins and cottars on the other – as lawyers found it convenient to suppose. An enterprising villein quickly got hold of additional land, for which he paid rent like a freeman, while continuing to perform services for his original virgate. An enterprising lord soon found it advantageous to commute some services for cash payments, especially perhaps on a manor remote from his normal place of residence. Though the amount of this commutation fluctuated from year to year as well as from manor to manor, in a long period of prosperity two factors told steadily in its favour. As soon as villeins were able to sell part of their own crops for money, they had resources which they would normally be eager to expend for this purpose, as the lord's bailiff was no doubt frequently reminded. At the same time, the bailiff knew how true was the dictum, 'Customary tenants neglect their work.' On a big estate which had many villeins, the enforcement of week-work might still be a regrettable necessity; on a small one, where the demesne servants had always had a considerable share in the working of the land, the bailiff might advise his master to dispense as much as possible with the grudging efforts of the villeins, except probably at harvest-time.

In the early part of the fourteenth century, however, for reasons which are still obscure, agricultural prices fell, so that the period of expansion on the land came to an end. This might mean an increase in the commutation of labour services on some big estates, where the demesne was now leased out to a single farmer instead. But on small ones the lord might react to financial difficulties by going back completely to the old system, under which he got his demesne cultivated by his villeins without having to pay cash wages. Perhaps we shall not be far from the truth if we conclude that, when Edward III declared war on France in 1337, his subjects in country districts were still predominantly villeins and cottars performing regular labour services, but in most of these districts sufficient services had been commuted, though usually on a partial and temporary basis, for freedom from service to have become a widespread aspiration.

The Black Death

In August 1348 the Black Death came across the Channel, a more formidable foe than any invading army. In its pneumonic form it was spread by direct contagion, in the bubonic by fleas from the body of the black rat. A succinct account by an eyewitness says:

> It passed most rapidly from place to place, swiftly killing ere mid-day many who in the morning had been well, and without respect of persons (some few rich people excepted), not permitting those destined to die to live more than three, or at most four days.

After about a year, the epidemic passed away northwards into Scotland, but there were at least three smaller visitations in the same generation. This had a cumulative effect in killing off the children born directly after the original calamity, and largely explains the astonishing long-term effect of the Black Death. According to the best modern authority, by the end of the century the population of the island had been halved and it took almost two hundred years to recover its former total.[1]

The immediate impact was probably greatest in the congested, undrained streets of towns: Bristol, for instance, lost fully one-third of its inhabitants. But there were individual villages which fared even worse. At Steeple Barton, Oxfordshire, in 1349–50, it was recorded that 32 of the 36 customary tenants were dead, the water-mill lay in ruins, and more than 600 acres were uncultivated.

[1] J. C. Russell: *British Medieval Population,* pp. 236, 270 and 272

And things became worse rather than better, for four years later the manor-house was described as 'worth nothing' and the number of uncultivated acres had doubled. At Tilgarsley in the same county, which before the plague had had 52 tenants, the desolation was complete, for in 1359 a tax-collector reported that no-one had lived there for the past nine years. Many villages, in fact, were lost, disappearing from the records, never to be lived in again. In our own days, however, some have been rediscovered from the air, the outline of street and field cutting right across present paths and hedges, and the strips, where once the oxen struggled, still clearly visible. Occasionally the ruins of a church survive to remind us of the people who once lived and worked within the sound of its bell.

Altogether, in the period between 1350 and 1550 about a thousand villages disappeared; remains of their ground plans can be found in most of the southern and midland counties – a hundred of them, for instance, in Warwickshire alone. But the length of the period, during which these villages passed one by one from knowledge, shows that their disappearance was due to other causes besides the Black Death. A high proportion were deliberately destroyed by landlords who found that the new shortage of labour made other sorts of farming far more profitable than the tillage of the open fields, which needed so many men to carry out its traditional tasks.

Decline of Villeinage

It was here, in the shortage of labourers caused by the plague, that the peasant came to acquire a new value. In direct proportion as the population dropped, every surviving peasant, and the work he did, rose in importance. Where once he had pleaded he could now demand. The villein could press for commutation of labour services into rent, with the expectation of something better than the piecemeal temporary concessions of the past. Yet, in the changed conditions of the Black Death world, for the villein to offer rent instead of work was to present his lord with a very disadvantageous proposal. Hired labour had become both scarce and expensive, so that villein labour was more valuable than ever before. Manorial lords therefore tried to hold on to the duties their villeins owed them and to resist the greater bargaining power of the peasant. Where lords were particularly obstinate, their villeins simply ran away, to the towns or to other manors, where a new master would be glad to pay wages to any extra worker. In the records of the manor court of Rotherfield Peppard in Oxfordshire for 1351, two such fugitives are named:

> The jury present that William Seman, villein of the lady of the manor . . . and Gilbert Bolle . . . are born bondsmen of the lady but live outside her lordship. So their nearest relations are ordered to make them come and live within the lordship by the time of the next court . . .

It is plain from later references in the same records that these villeins did not come back, which is not surprising in view of the great competition for workers of all kinds. Something similar happened in 1390 at Theydon Garnon in Essex, where it was recorded that

> Simon Jakeboy withdrew John Pretylwell from the service of Thomas Mason into his own service in the occupation of malt-monger, giving him 26s. 8d. and food and clothing every year . . . which John Pretylwell formerly was a ploughman.

And on the fenland estates of Crowland Abbey bondmen were absconding at the rate of one a year throughout the whole period from 1365 to 1400.

Since those villeins who did not run away could intersperse their rendering of services with minor acts of sabotage and sit-down strikes (to which the records also bear witness), the long-term result was bound to be the triumph of commutation. By the close of the century even the traditionally conservative estates of the Church were rapidly giving way on this issue. But a kind of last-ditch struggle remained to be fought over the marks of villein status, which were in principle unaffected by the termination of villein labour. Such payments as merchet and heriot were still legally due to the lord who kept track of his villein families, and it was not until the Tudor period that their exaction came entirely to an end. The big new class of rent-paying tenants, however, were for the most part soon regarded as entirely free persons – especially by those lords who had been prompt in re-organizing their manors to suit a new world where labour was scarce.

Some lords sold their demesne land outright, but the commonest practice was to let it out, preferably to a single big farmer, who might be attracted by the offer of a stock-and-land lease. Even the great abbots began to do this, though they might still provide for the needs of their own monks and dependants by requiring rent to be paid in terms of food. If only a part of the demesne was let out, the lord's need of villein labour-services was at any rate proportionately reduced, and he could make do with wage-earners, such as were also required on the farms of the rising class of substantial lease-holders and other tenants.

The Rural Wage-earner

There had always been some people about the manor who worked for wages. Specialists, such as the shepherd, ploughman, carpenter, and blacksmith, may by the thirteenth century have been earning a reasonable wage. But the unskilled labour of cottar families and the younger sons of villeins, which must have been in plentiful supply (and perhaps for that very reason is seldom mentioned in manorial records), was no doubt ill-requited from time immemorial by small doles of food or smaller still in cash. But the Black Death had transformed the position. However humble his social status, the wage-earner was now scarce and in increasing demand: he wished to see his value represented in good money terms.

To some employers it seemed to be the end of all things, when such demands were made. So thought a certain John Gower, poet and lord of two manors, of whom we shall hear more later:[1]

The world goeth fast from bad to worse, when shepherd and cowherd demand more for their labour than the master-bailiff was wont to take in days gone by. Labour is now at so high a price that he who will order his business aright must pay five or

[1] See p. 180

six shillings now for what cost two in former times. Labourers of old were not wont to eat of wheaten bread; their meat was of beans or coarser corn, and their drink of water alone . . . then was the world ordered aright for folk of this sort . . . Three things, all of the same sort, are merciless when they get the upper hand; a water-flood, a wasting fire, and the common multitude of small folk. For these will never be checked by reason or discipline . . .

Parliament shared his sentiments, to which it gave practical expression in the Statute of Labourers of 1351. This ordered labourers of all kinds to accept the wage-rates which had existed before the Black Death, forbade them to move about the country in search of better conditions, and instituted 'justices of labourers' to enforce the law.

Prices

To modern eyes, of course, all the wages that we find carefully recorded in bailiffs' manorial accounts appear absurdly small:

For the smith's wage for maintaining the iron parts of ploughs this year 20s., besides 3 bushels of wheat as extra.

One carpenter hired to mend carts for $7\frac{1}{2}$ days at 5d. a day.

For reaping and binding 2 acres of rye 2s.

At all times, however, wages only make sense when set beside prices, on which the effect of the Black Death was by no means uniform. They rose very sharply in the very first years of crisis, but over a longer period of a century or more there is a contrast between the rise in manufactured goods (such as nails, for instance) which went up by three-quarters, and general foodstuffs, which went up by only one-quarter. In the particular case of wheat, although its price fluctuated wildly according to the state of the harvest, the average in 1400–1449 was almost exactly the same as in 1300–1349. Indeed, the depressed state of the market would have produced an actual fall in agricultural prices, but for depreciation of the coinage: by 1412 the penny contained only two-thirds of its former standard content of silver.

Rise of the Yeoman Class

Meanwhile wages, though held in check for a time by the Statute of Labourers, had approximately doubled. This gave a further incentive to changes in the use of land. The stock-and-land leaseholder of the demesne, as previously noticed, would suffer with all other substantial farmers from this rise in the cost of labour: hence a new interest on his part in sheep-grazing. In the centuries between Hastings and the Black Death, abbots and other great lords had been the typical breeders of sheep: flocks numbering tens of thousands were often a feature of the intensive farming practised on their big estates. Now it was the day of the smaller man.

Yet it was not altogether easy to turn land over to the raising of sheep, especially where it lay scattered among the ancient arable strips in the open fields. Here, the immemorial routine of seedtime and harvest, and the throwing open of the fields to the beasts of the villagers at fixed intervals, made any innovation difficult. A long process of complicated bargaining might, indeed, make it possible to consolidate a large holding of strips either by exchange with other strip-holders or by purchase; a lucky inheritance might also help. Then the holding could be enclosed and turned over to pasture: but such consolidation was rare in the fourteenth century and not very common later on. Demesne land, however, which is sometimes the basis of the 'manor farm' of modern times, was often handed over in a single block, readily adaptable to new uses.

But pasture farming developed chiefly in the hilly areas, outside the traditional manorial system. Here, along the borders of Wales and Scotland, in the north-west and along the Pennines, the manorial system had never taken much root; the soil was so poor that harvesters went every year to earn a few weeks' wages in the more fertile south. Here the closely-knit manor was the exception and the villein with his scattered virgate something of a rarity. So the land was more freely available as a start – and the labour, too,

162   THE CHANGING VILLAGE

to take advantage of the new opportunities. In these areas there had been little in the way of labour services for a lord and far less resistance to the commuting of those there were. With vested interests less entrenched in these parts than others, new agricultural ideas could be adopted. On the hilly moors of Britain the sheep was to be monarch of all he surveyed.

In these years, therefore, the land-holding class was greatly enlarged, as prosperous peasants took advantage of their opportunities to climb into it. From the start there were some well placed to do so – in particular, the manor reeve. Originally, he had been elected annually by his fellow-villeins to be their representative before the lord and to act as their overseer in the work performed. By 1300, however, he was beginning to become a hereditary official and therefore was in a strong position to push his interests. He would gain commutation of his labour services and buy – or marry into possession of – free land, helped by the fact that he best knew his lord's intentions. And other peasants rose too, adding other men's land to their own and getting the lord's permission to make intakes from the woods and hold them at low rents. The members of this very important rising group began to be known sometimes as 'franklins' or 'yeomen'.

However, not all peasants rose to prosperity: some were deprived of their lands by those more pushing or by the more impersonal processes of marriage and sub-division among heirs. Such men became wage-earners, either on other men's land and in general employment about the village; or in the towns, as saddlers, carters, thatchers, butchers, tailors and so on; or they found a living in the cloth industry, where there were now many specialized occupations. Smith and Taylor, Weaver and Walker, may be instanced as significantly common surnames, which date from the period when it first became desirable to add to the Bible name or saint's name given invariably at baptism: this had been enough for identification in smaller and less mobile communities.

The Peasants' Revolt

The fourteenth century, it should by now be plain, was one of deep social change, even though swifter in some parts of the country than others. So far it may seem that most of it came about quietly in spite of the strains involved – or that the strains were not in fact great. Yet in June 1381 a large part of England was shaken by the Peasants' Revolt, in which the insurgents of Kent and Essex entered London under Wat Tyler, who was perhaps an ex-soldier; the Tower was captured, and the Archbishop of Canterbury and the Treasurer were murdered. Although there was pillaging of property in many counties, sheer poverty was not the main cause: Froissart, in fact, spoke of 'the ease and riches that the common people were of, which moved them to this rebellion'.

At least four things went into the mixing-bowl of revolt at this time. First, there was the unevenness of the changes within the manorial system – the reluctance of many lords to accept the new liberties demanded by their villeins. The revolt blazed mainly in the south and east, which were substantially the parts of England where the manor was most highly organized. Here commutation of services was slowest, the strip system of agriculture most fixed, and the opportunities for peasants to acquire free land and work it in their own way were most restricted. At every focal point of the revolt the peasants demanded the abolition of villeinage and the surrender of the manor rolls on which their customary services were written. 'They tried to burn all records', writes a St Albans monk, 'and killed all who could record past or current events. It was dangerous to be known as a clerk and worse still to be found carrying an inkhorn.'

Secondly, the wealth of the Church and even its doctrines had recently been attacked by an Oxford scholar, John Wyclif, who was responsible for the first translation of the Bible into English. His followers, contemptuously known as 'lollards' (mutterers), were persecuted as heretics, but their movement survived down to the Reformation. Although Wyclif did not in any way encourage the peasants to revolt, the stand he had taken made it easier for other, more extreme religious reformers to come to the fore. This was particularly the case in Kent – a county where commutation was not a major issue. 'A crazy priest in the county of Kent, called John Ball,' said Froissart, 'was greatly instrumental in exciting these rebellious ideas'. And he goes on:

Every Sunday after mass, as the people were coming out of church, this John Ball was accustomed to assemble a crowd around him in the market-place and preach to them. On such occasions he would say, 'My good friends, matters cannot go on well in England until all things shall be in common; when there shall be neither vassals nor lords; when the lords shall be no more masters than ourselves . . . Are we not all descended from the same parents, Adam and Eve?'

John Ball's preaching provided a religious or moral justification for social and economic complaints, which gave the revolt some of the fervour of a crusade.

Thirdly, all these great tensions in society were heightened by the long miseries of a French war from which the glory had departed. Revolutions have often taken place against just such a background, for war tends to throw into relief all the social inequalities of peace. The Peasants' Revolt in England was preceded by something very similar in France.

But it was the poll tax of 1380 which precipitated the outbreak. Four years before, this had been a new tax, but it was becoming a regular feature of war finance: this was already the third imposition. Most previous taxes had left small men out of account, but this (as its name implies) was levied on every man's head, even though the richer were taxed more heavily. It seemed that the common people were unequal in everything but their liability to pay taxes, and this was the final grievance that made the revolutionary mixture complete.

Although the Revolt put an end to the poll tax, it did nothing to speed up the liberation from villeinage. If anything, it retarded it, for promises made by lords of manors at the height of the revolt were withdrawn quickly when once it collapsed; indeed, many lords explained the revolt to themselves as being the result of their too great kindness to their villeins. For a time, therefore, there was a renewed insistence upon labour services and reluctance to commute them. But in fact commutation had little to do with the kindness or unkindness of lords: it was the product of economic pressures and, once the panic of the revolt had worn off, the process was resumed.

Conditions in Scotland

In Scotland there were no earthquake-shocks of social discontent comparable with the Peasants' Revolt. But conditions there were quite different, even in the semi-Anglicized lowland areas – although the Black Death had struck in Scotland too. The social strains in England had been within the manorial system, but in Scottish agriculture there was nothing parallel to this. The peasantry were all tenants of a lord, or tenants of his tenants, and they often had to provide 'bondages', that is, perform specific tasks of ploughing, reaping, carrying, shearing, or peat-cutting. But they were nearly all free men, not tied to the land by a regular routine of week-work.

Rents were paid mostly in kind rather than money, and so were wages for farm labour. The circulation of money in Scotland was, in fact, very limited and farming was carried on almost entirely on a subsistence basis – that is, for the feeding of the farming family itself and of the lord, who often travelled round his estates to eat up his rents. The market had nothing like the same place in the ambitions of the Scottish peasant as with his English fellow, and this in itself is one of the reasons why money was slow to circulate – there was little demand for it. In England, as we have just seen, the demand for money largely transformed the manor.

Yet there were, in fact, great changes within Scottish society too. The long Wars of Independence (1286–1371) produced a dismal anarchy, in which the powers of the great lords multiplied and their demands on the peasants shifted in emphasis from economic to military obligations. In the Highlands especially, the clan system extended its hold and it even moved into the Lowlands. Private armies became a common thing, based not only upon the clan but upon 'manrent' forced by greater upon inferior chiefs. In the fifteenth century, the earl of Douglas burnt Stirling at the head of 600 men; a little later on, the earls of Huntly and Arran, taking their allies into account, were able to raise 6,500 and 7,500 men respectively. Such lords could threaten the throne itself, and on their own estates they wielded powers of life and death. Yet there was a certain mutual interest between the members of a clan, high and low, which did something to prevent the downright class legislation that England shows, for instance, in the Statute of Labourers.

Yet behind all this tumult the day-to-day business of the land went on: the permanent cultivation (made possible by constant manuring) of the in-field under oats and barley, and the more occasional farming of pieces taken in temporarily from the out-field. Except in the lowlands, stock-keeping was the most natural form of farming, with gorse and broom used as winter fodder to stave off the wretched necessity of killing off most of the cattle and sheep at Martinmas.

John Fordun, a fourteenth-century priest in Aberdeen, thus described the country of his birth:

Scotia has tracts of land bordering on the sea, pretty, level, and rich, with green meadows, and fertile and productive fields of corn and barley, and well adapted for growing beans, pease and all other produce . . . But in the upland districts, and along the highlands, the fields are less productive, except only in oats and barley. The country is there very hideous, interspersed with moors and marshy fields, muddy and dirty; it is, however, full of pasturage grass for cattle, and comely with verdure in the glens along the water-courses. This region abounds in wool-bearing sheep, and in horses, and its soil is grassy, feeds cattle and wild beasts, is rich in milk and wool, and manifold in its wealth of fish.

For the growth of industrial wealth, however, we must return to England.

13

CRAFTS AND CRAFTSMEN

SMALL-SCALE handicrafts, such as the work of the carpenter, cobbler, and blacksmith, formed an important part of village and still more of town life from very early times. But there are at least two reasons why they attract more attention towards the close of the Middle Ages. In the fourteenth and fifteenth centuries the profitable export trade in raw wool was being turned into something still more profitable, namely the export of woollen cloth, the making of which continued until the Industrial Revolution to be the largest, most widespread, and most profitable of all English industries. This, as we shall see, employed a great many different types of craftsmen, often in what had been rural localities. During the same period, the general trade of many towns was reaching a size which made it a convenient arrangement for supervision by a single merchant gild to give place to the supervision of the affairs of each craft by its own separate craft gild. In its heyday this institution, of which a relic survives in the names of the London Companies, had much social value and interest.

We may take the growth of the woollen industry first, since this in some measure affected the entire population. Even today there are reminders of its past pre-eminence, such as the woolsack which forms the seat of the lord chancellor in the house of lords or the outstanding size and magnificence of some medieval parish churches, such as Cirencester, in the wool-working areas. 'Spinster' shows how unmarried women were expected to spend their time, and we all use without thinking phrases which get their meaning from the processes of the woollen industry – 'to spin a yarn', 'to unravel a mystery', 'to be on tenterhooks'. As for contemporary opinion, we may quote the parliament of 1454, which declared: 'The making of cloth within all parts of the realm is the greatest occupation and living of the poor commons of this land.'

167

The Wool Trade

Mention has already been made of the increase in the proportion of wool grown by peasant sheep farmers. Since they did not necessarily pay wages to shepherds or sink much capital in their sheep-runs, they could often tide over bad times more easily than the large landowners. Having sheared his own sheep and washed the wool in the long summer days, the peasant slung it on the backs of one or two packhorses and himself urged them along the narrow tracks to the nearest market. But this did not necessarily bring him into contact with the foreign merchant, who had been accustomed to do big deals with big men. Hence the emergence of a new type of middleman, the 'woolman' or 'brogger' (broker), who rode round the villages at shearing time and bought up the clip for subsequent sale to the foreigner. Some of them came from London, which was increasingly the centre of the trade, but many came also from the wool-growing counties. In Lincolnshire there

Plate 25. *Carrying the corn uphill.* From the Luttrell Psalter. This is just such a straining cart as Chaucer spoke of in 'The Friar's Tale' (Nevill Coghill edition (Penguin), *Canterbury Tales*, p. 318):

> They saw a farm-cart loaded up with hay.
> There was a carter driving, but the way
> Was deep and muddy and the cart stood still.
> The carter lashed and shouted with a will,
> 'Hey, Brock! Hup, Scottie! Never mind for stones!
> The foul fiend come and fetch you, flesh and bones!

(Cf. text pp. 154–5.)

Plate 26. *A deserted village.* Middle Ditchford in Gloucestershire: in 1491 it was spoken of as having fairly recently decayed. The village streets can be seen, and the ditches separating the cottages and their plots of land – though the cottages themselves have left no trace. Round the village are the remains of the open-field strips. (Cf. text p. 157.)

Plate 27. *Weaving.* This picture, dating from about 1300, shows the important advances made in weaving during the 12th and 13th centuries. The warp lies horizontally between the warp beam, farthest from the weaver, and the cloth beam in front of her. Alternate warp threads pass through one or other of the two sets of 'healds', suspended from wooden slats, which are raised and lowered by the foot treadles, to make a gap (the 'shed'), through which the weft-shuttle travels. The weaver in the picture is holding the 'reed', which sweeps down the weft against the cloth, building up in front of her. When needed, more warp can be paid out from the warp beam and the cloth wound on to the cloth beam. The horizontal set-up, the healds, the reed and the cloth beam, are all developments of this time. (Cf. text pp. 170–1.)

Plate 25

Plate 26

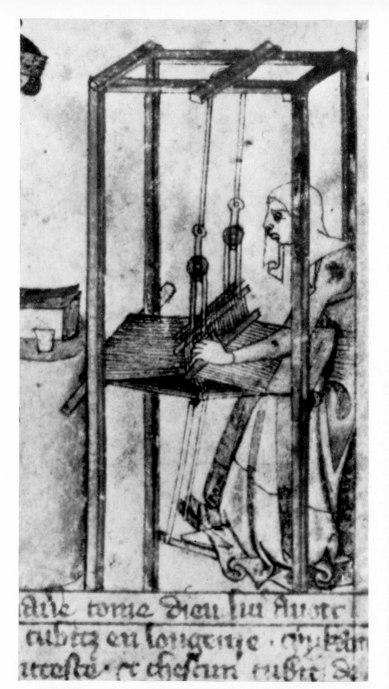

dnie tonie dieu lui fuote
cubitz en longenie · cin kin
icasste · et chescun cubit de

Plate 27

was one who left money to the churches of thirty different parishes
in which he had traded. In the Cotswolds they can be traced by
their tomb-brasses: solemn in death, they lie with their feet on
wool-sacks or on sheep, in seemingly ironic imitation of the
heraldic burials of their betters. Yet some of them climbed
into the aristocracy, as did William Grevil, 'flower of the wool
merchants of all England', whose descendants became earls of
Warwick.

In the reign of Edward I the amount of wool exported was about
30,000 sacks a year, a figure which remained fairly constant until
1350. He imposed the so-called Ancient Custom, a duty of 6s .8d.
upon a sack which fetched anything between £3 10s. and £12. This
and other later duties were collected at the ports through which the
wool passed, restricted for convenience to a certain number of
'staple towns'. These in turn became limited to Calais, an early
capture in the Hundred Years War and one which remained in
English hands for two centuries. For most of this long period the
Company of the Staple of Calais, recruited originally from wool-
shippers in general but becoming increasingly a London organization, collected the export duties and paid them over to the
exchequer, not without some advantage for themselves on the way.
The Italians secured exemption by an expensive licence, but by
1400 three-quarters of the wool exported passed through English
hands. The woolmen bought the required grades of wool and wool-
fells (sheepskins with wool adhering) and conveyed the bales to the
ports for shipment. The Staplers then took it to Calais, where duty
was paid and sale organized, either to foreign buyers on the spot or
by sending round to the great continental fairs.

For a time the wool merchants cut a big figure: both as individuals and as a company they helped with the financing of the
Hundred Years War – and a number of them went bankrupt in
consequence. But the war also occasioned some immigration of
highly skilled Flemish weavers to England in search of better
opportunities, and a series of experiments in taxation which ended
in a charge of one-third on the value of all wool exported; this
was designed to give a stimulus to exports of cloth instead.
Conditions at home and abroad now favoured the momentous
change by which the English began to reap a double profit as wool

G

growers and as woollen manufacturers, able to charge the foreigners both for a valuable raw material and for the labour which worked it up into cloth. By 1400 the number of sacks of wool exported had been reduced by half, and the 15,000 sacks of 1400 had fallen to 10,000 by 1485. Meanwhile, the export of cloths (24 yards long and 63 inches wide) had risen from an annual total of 5,000 to something in excess of 50,000.

Processes in Cloth-making

As early as the twelfth century there had been good sales abroad for the fine cloths of the eastern counties, made in such centres as Lincoln, Louth, Stamford, Beverley, and York. Common cloth for home wear had been made, however, in all parts of the country, so it was easy for the export trade now to spread into new areas – those in which a good quality of wool was conveniently near; places where the Flemish weavers settled and would share their trade secrets; and especially, hilly western districts which had streams to turn the wheel for a fulling-mill. But at this stage it will make the picture clearer if some explanation is given of the main processes in an industry which counted altogether upon fourteen types of worker to handle the wool, between the sheep's back and that of its eventual wearer.

To begin with, the wool had to be thoroughly washed and cleaned. Then there was the 'carding', a process in which the material was passed between two pieces of wood, rather like butter pats but having a number of small iron spikes embedded in their surface: by moving them in opposite directions, short wool was effectively disentangled. The long wool for worsted was combed instead, with a pair of large, heated combs, one of which was fastened to a post. Next came the spinning, which was women's work, done with distaff and spindle or – after about 1300 – with the more convenient spinning-wheel. This turned the fibres into a continuous twisted yarn ready for the weaver.

So far as the weaving process is concerned, textiles have been made since remote antiquity by what is in essentials the same process. A series of fixed threads, known as the warp, is set up running the length of the loom, and the weaver interlaces these with a continuous thread, the weft, which he passes to and fro between his outstretched arms. To produce this result, the warp threads are attached in two alternate series to two cords or wires called 'healds'; these are lifted in turn, so as to form a shed through which the weaver passes the weft on a shuttle. Thus the interlacing is achieved at high speed, with brief pauses to pack the lines of weft together more closely with a batten (the 'reed'), and the completed cloth is wound on to a beam placed immediately in front of the weaver as he sits at work. The chief limiting factor was that the cloth could not be made wider than the span of a man's arms when contracted sufficiently to throw the shuttle; broadcloth, which was $1\frac{3}{4}$ yards wide after shrinking, could only be woven by two weavers seated side by side.

The woven cloth had next to be fulled – that is, shrunk, felted and scoured by being put into water with fuller's earth and beaten. In early times this was done simply by immersing it in a large bowl and treading or 'walking' it with bare feet – a most tiring process, especially if the cloth were a large piece, when it could take two whole days. Some time in the twelfth century fulling mills reached England from the continent: a water wheel operated two heavy wooden mallets, which thudded alternately into the cloth as it lay soaking in a trough. Mills no doubt spread slowly at first, but after a hundred years or so they were important enough to influence the location of the whole cloth industry.

The fulled cloth was next taken into the open and stretched and dried upon a 'tenter', a wooden framework of posts and beams which was covered with small tenterhooks to hold the cloth firmly. When dry the cloth was removed from the tenters and put upon a table to be examined for flaws, as many imperfections as possible being taken out with small tweezers.

Unless the cloth had been already 'dyed in the wool', this process would constitute the next stage. Some cloth, indeed, was sent undyed to the Low Countries which, after the growth of the English cloth industry had challenged their own weaving, made a speciality of the finishing of cloth. Still, a good deal was dyed in England, the cloth being dropped into large vats of dye (which was sometimes heated) and stirred about by men wielding large poles. The most common colour was blue, for which the dye was woad, mainly imported from Gascony and Germany, and there was also a dull red made from madder roots; this was brought largely from the Netherlands to be sold, for instance, in the Maddermarket at Norwich. Fine scarlet came from cochineal, yellow from weld, and less pure yellows and browns from native lichens.

The two final stages of cloth-making were teasing and shearing. The former was the raising of the nap of the cloth by stroking it with teasels, the heads of a thistle-like plant then cultivated for the purpose. In the fifteenth century, if not earlier, this process also could be worked by water-power in a 'gig-mill', where the teasels whirled round on rollers. The shearing corrected the teasing process, clipping off sections of the nap that had been raised too high with sharp, flat-ended shears about eighteen inches long.

Among the various improvements introduced in this flourishing industry, the one that had the most far-reaching effects was the fulling-mill. Those thunderous hammers could only do their work if the industry moved towards the streams that gave them power. Gradually therefore the centre of the cloth industry moved from the eastern plains into the west and parts of the north – especially to counties west and south-west of the Cotswolds, which towards the end of the fifteenth century produced half the cloth. The big shift of locality helped the English industry to escape from the restrictions imposed on free enterprise in the older chartered towns, which gave it an advantage over the ancient urban centres of cloth-making on the continent. The Flemish industry also suffered a technical handicap, since it had no water-power available to turn the fulling-mills.

There were regional differences in the types of cloth woven. The Cotswolds and west Wiltshire were famous for fine broadcloths, as was Somerset for Mendips cloth. Yorkshire and the north-west were noted for coarser materials; the Welsh border had its Ludlow cloth; lightweight Kerseys and high quality Worsteds took their names from two East Anglian villages. These cloths, produced in particular regions, tended to be sent abroad from particular ports: Bristol for the west of England and the Welsh border, Hull for Yorkshire and the north, but London for the whole country.

The Rise of the Clothier

As regards the organization of the cloth industry and methods of marketing, the existence of so many stages in manufacture would be likely to lead to one of two results. Either small men would attempt to carry out every process under their own roof, with the result that production remained small-scale; or larger men would emerge, setting whole villages to work and controlling the entire manufacture on a much wider basis with a view to more effective and more profitable competition in foreign markets. In fact, both developments occurred – the activity of the small man preceding that of the large.

The small man might himself have begun as a weaver, buying small quantities of wool at the local market and bringing them home to his wife to be spun. He would set up the warp on his own loom and weave a narrow cloth to the limits of the yarn available. He would full it himself, treading it in a bowl as the Romans had done, and might even dye it if he could buy woad or other dye-stuffs locally. Eventually he would sell it at the market, either to some small merchant or to a tailor. If things went well, he would start to expand: he would buy or make another loom and perhaps contract for a small but regular supply of wool from a local grower. His whole family would take part in the enterprise – the children carding the wool, his wife at the spinning-wheel, he himself at one loom and an assistant at another. He would load the cloth on the back of the horse and send his eldest son with it to the local fulling-mill. In the same way he might send the cloth out to be dyed, and then divide up the rest of the finishing jobs among the family.

Gradually he would expand further still. He would take his wool as it came in from the grower to other cottages in the village to be carded and spun, and in turn deliver the spun thread to yet other families to be woven. He could now send a fairly large quantity of cloth to be fulled and dyed, and would need to buy extra pack-horses. By this time he might possibly send his cloth to a gig-mill to be 'raised', and it would be sent out again to be sheared over the table. When this long course of development, which might well take more than one generation, was successfully completed the result was the emergence of a 'clothier', a person who organized cloth production for the market.

The clothier was clearly a capitalist employer, for whom many of his poorer neighbours worked and on whom they might become completely dependent for work and wages. Eventually, they might depend on him for the very looms they used and the houses they lived in. Some of them might even be brought to work together under one roof, both for greater speed and efficiency and so that a check could be kept upon the various frauds that might be practised. And for his part the clothier would want to bring more and more of the production processes under his own management, by buying up dyeing vats, fulling- and gig-mills. He might even become a landowner and grow the wool he needed. Such a man was John Tame in the mid-fifteenth century, who kept flocks on his estates at Fairford to supply his large-scale manufacture of cloth in Cirencester.

The Export of Cloth

When they controlled so much, it is surprising that clothiers did not themselves, as a general rule, take part in the export trade. The long lines of their packhorses led to the local markets, to the more distant fairs, and ultimately to the ports, where the cloth was sold both to English and foreign traders. At the markets and fairs it was often bought up by the drapers, who specialized in the selling of cloth. And at the ports, more than to any others, it was sold to the English Merchant Adventurers. These were merchants whose interests were by no means confined to cloth: some of them might be staplers as well, engaged in the Calais trade, and others were wine importers. In fact, Adventurers were originally distinguished from Staplers as being all-round traders, who literally ventured their wealth on things more risky than the organized wool monopoly. Wool, however, began to be heavily taxed, as we have already noticed, and the export of cloth took its place as the trade in which men-on-the-make engaged. Thus the Merchant Adventurers began to concentrate more and more upon the export of cloth, and became the main customers of the clothiers. There were groups of these Adventurers in the more important trading towns round the coast, from Newcastle upon Tyne to Bristol. But by 1500 the London group had become dominant and claimed supremacy in the title they adopted – 'the Merchant Adventurers of England'; their trade at that time was concentrated upon Antwerp.

In the ships of the Merchant Adventurers battling into the Baltic or making their way up the Scheldt on the tide, we have one end of the spun-out thread of wool production. The other was held in the rough hands of the shepherd guarding his sheep in the windy fields. Well might a thirteenth-century writer advise on the sort of man this solitary protector should be:

> It profiteth the lord to have discreet shepherds, watchful and kindly, so that the sheep be not tormented by their wrath but crop their pasture in peace and joyfulness; for it is a token of the shepherd's kindness if the sheep be not scattered abroad but browse around him in company. Let him provide himself with a good barkable dog and lie nightly with his sheep.

In view of the importance of their trade, it is not surprising that weavers were apparently the first group of craftsmen to set up their own organization in rivalry with the merchant gild, which claimed to control every handicraft. In London the weavers soon after 1100 had the protection of a royal charter, and the city authorities eventually offered the king a large sum for its withdrawal. Winchester, Oxford, Huntingdon, Lincoln, and York are other towns which are known to have had gilds of weavers at an early date. At Leicester in the thirteenth century they were prosecuted for 'making by themselves a provision about weaving against the community of the gild merchant'. By the fourteenth century, however, when the establishment of craft gilds of all kinds became acceptable to the authorities of most well-established boroughs, much of the weaving (as we have seen) had followed the fulling into new areas, with the result that weavers' gilds lost their original prominence.

Most craft gilds were very small affairs, as is evident from the fact that moderate-sized towns might have as many as 20, while York had 41, seven of which had no more than 77 members among them. In London half a dozen 'great companies', such as the drapers and goldsmiths, consisted entirely of merchants, but in most places the typical craft gild was made up of men who worked with their own hands or at least served in their own shop: in managing their trade affairs they remained under the ultimate control of the wealthiest of their fellow-citizens, who now ruled the town through a chartered corporation rather than the outmoded merchant gild.

It was the recognized duty of a craft gild to control the quality and methods of production of the article in which its members traded, from bread to boots, from butchers' meat to saddlery, from cutlery to tailoring. At Bristol, for example, 'If any trader ruin by his evil working a cloth or garment to him delivered to be cut, and the possessor complain to the master and wardens' of the gild, he will be required to make good the loss, 'so every trader shall be better advised to cut well and sufficiently the cloth that is delivered unto him'. The gild officials inspected workshops, tested the skill of newcomers to the trade, and frowned on night work, which might provide cover for fraud.

Prices, on the other hand, were regarded in principle as the concern of national or borough authorities; the former fixed sliding-scales for bread and ale, the latter were usually ready to hear complaints about extortion in any trade. But there is no doubt that craft gilds enforced minimum prices upon their members and put them up from time to time by private agreement. Such activities were normally concealed in order to avoid public outcry and interference from the mayor, but in Coventry we know that the barbers in the 1390's agreed to raise their prices, 'making the cost of that art so much dearer to the damage of the whole people', and half a century later the London shearmen had definite regulations, such as 'For shearing of scarlet and all other engrained cloth, every yard twopence'.

Journeymen and Apprentices

So far we have considered only the interests of master-craftsmen, but the membership of a craft gild also included skilled employees or 'journeymen' and apprentices under training. Wages, like prices, might be imposed upon the gildsmen from above, but agreement on wages and conditions of employment was, at least to begin with, made and enforced inside the typical craft gild without serious difficulty. This was partly because custom, including the customary relationship between superior and inferior crafts, changed very slowly. But another very important reason lay in the fact that the journeyman usually expected to be only temporarily a wage-earner, until he found a good chance to set up his own business. He therefore had less interest in driving up rates of wages which he might be required to pay to his own journeyman later on.

The system of apprenticeship had a double significance. As a method of industrial training in days when there were no technical schools or colleges, it had much to recommend it. Its duration, fixed in London at seven years, was sufficient for learning both the craft itself and the allied skill of handling the customer. Though it was made difficult for the apprentice to change employer, the gild officials kept an eye on his progress and in some trades he was required eventually to prove his skilfulness by submitting a 'masterpiece'. But apprenticeship was also an effective means of restricting entry to the trade, both by limiting the numbers apprenticed and (in some more desirable occupations) by charging a fee to the apprentice's parents. The conditions were in any case arduous, for he resided with his master, had no set hours of work, and was entitled to nothing except his keep and clothing. 'He must do all servile offices about the house and be obedient to all his master's commandments, and shall suffer such correction as his master shall think meet.'

Social Activities; the Plays

Nevertheless, there is a pleasant atmosphere of social democracy about the craft gild, with its elected master, wardens, and council; its provision of relief for sick, poor, and aged members; and its emphasis upon the value of belonging, as three of Chaucer's Canterbury pilgrims did, to 'a solemn and great fraternity'. Many trades had a patron saint, such as the shoemakers' St Crispin or the Bishop Blaize of the woolcombers, and nearly all spent part of their common fund in religious observances of some kind. Across the centuries we perhaps come closest to these bustling, small-scale societies of shopkeepers and artisans, whose members once thronged the narrow streets of our older towns, if we think of them, not in their capacity as makers and purveyors of commodities, but as the long-silenced actors and audiences which for two hundred years kept up the annual pageant and excitement of the mystery plays.

These were religious plays – 'mystery' being here a corruption of the Latin *ministerium* or service – produced on the Feast of Corpus Christi or ten days earlier, at Whitsun. The subjects were taken from familiar Bible stories, and each brief play – with plenty of knock-about action – was shown on a wheeled platform, which was halted for performances at suitable places in the streets. Each gild offered its own production, choosing if possible an appropriate theme. Carpenters or, better still, shipwrights would be seen building Noah's ark; the goldsmiths might show the Three Wise Men with their rich offerings; some part of the woollen industry might claim a vested interest in the shepherds with their flocks at Bethlehem; and the armourers equip the knights whom Herod sends for the slaughter of the Innocents. Since few gildsmen could read, the text originally provided by priest or monk must have been handed down at first by word of mouth, and was no doubt freely adapted to suit the actors' tastes. But there was intense rivalry among the gilds in equipping their plays with permanent collections of gorgeous costumes, effective stage 'props', and imaginative devices to represent such popular settings as the grinning mouth of hell. Our modern word 'pageant' once meant the wheeled platform on which these splendours were displayed.

By the time of Shakespeare this type of play had fallen largely into disuse. In 1570, for instance, the records of the Norwich grocers show that their once fine pageant wagon had been left out in the open until it was 'so weather beaten that the chief part was rotten'. The craft gilds, too, had lost much of their medieval character. Some, like the London livery companies, became exclusive associations of rich merchants, divorced in most cases from any craft. Others hived off journeymen or yeomen gilds, which struggled to maintain the separate interests of wage-earners who could no longer afford to set up their own businesses. Even in the smaller towns, gilds raised their fees and ruthlessly exploited their monopoly position. But the craft gilds had served medieval urban society well and helped its growth.

Plight of Unskilled Labourers

In speaking of urban society, however, it is all too easy to forget its poorest elements, about whom the records have little to tell. The unskilled labourers, who did rough tasks of carrying, hauling, and cleaning and all the other unpleasant odd jobs around the workshop, did not normally belong to any gild. It is possible to infer something about their numbers from the situation in London: every gildsman had the 'freedom of the city', yet at the close of the Middle Ages three-quarters of the Londoners were not citizens. Miners and masons, who formed the two big groups of organized handicraftsmen outside the towns, were also assisted by a mass of unskilled workers, such as the men who in Edward I's reign broke up stone in the Dorsetshire quarries for $1\frac{1}{2}$d. or 2d. a day and the women who carried it away for even less. Broadly speaking, unskilled were paid a little more than half as much as skilled workers, so long as they retained their full physical strength and trade was flourishing. In bad times – and often also as the result of sickness, accident or the onset of old age – the plight of the unskilled industrial worker must have been even worse than that of the cottar families in the countryside, which were always the first to feel bitter want.

Medieval men were not lacking in Christian charity: even King John was sufficiently concerned to provide a daily portion of bread and gruel for more than two thousand paupers in London and the provinces. Beggars, often hideously maimed or disfigured by leprosy, would not have been such a common feature of the medieval street scene if it had not been usual for those who could to give them something. But in every period of dearth, civil disturbance, or plague those who normally lived on the very margin of subsistence, especially the very young and the very old, provided a problem with which society was unable to cope. The slow rate at which population recovered from the Black Death and its after-effects is one of the most striking general facts about the life of the later Middle Ages, and the contemporary books to which we shall turn in our final chapter contain no comment more apt than this from *Piers Plowman*: 'Pitiful is it to read the cottage woman's woe.'

14

THE ENGLAND OF THE CANTERBURY TALES
AND PASTON LETTERS

WE have already surveyed the medieval scene in different aspects. Let us look at it once more, through the eyes of men who actually experienced it. This only begins to be possible towards the end of the Middle Ages, when the writing of books ceased to be the virtual monopoly of cloistered monks and instead laymen, who had closer contacts with everyday life, took up the pen. The world of every day is portrayed for us by three poets, Chaucer, Gower, and Langland, and still more directly in the letters of the Paston family, preoccupied with the management of their various estates.

With the exception of Langland, the viewpoint of all these men is upper middle class: they look at the world as from the fringes of the Court and have a natural liking for stability and order. They fear both aristocratic anarchy above them and mass unrest below them, such as was revealed in the Peasants' Revolt of 1381 and that of Jack Cade seventy years later. Look for a moment at Chaucer's lively group of pilgrims jogging their way through the orchards and villages between London and Canterbury: there is hardly a really poor man among them. But there are a knight and a prioress, a squire and a man of law, a merchant and a physician – respectable people on well-shod horses who express the thoughts of their own class. Their language is rather cautious, breathing suspicion of any change as likely to be for the worse. They think as John Gower did in the reign of Richard II:

> *King Richard's sixteenth year it is;*
> *And what will happen after this,*
> *God knows – for men see nowadays,*

Whichever way they turn their gaze,
The world so changed and overthrown
That it is well-nigh upside down
Compared with days of long ago.

Writers of English

Geoffrey Chaucer is buried in Westminster Abbey, so that even in death he does not lie far from the centres of power. His life too revolved round those centres throughout its sixty-year course from 1340 to 1400. He was brought up as a page in the household of the wife of one of the sons of Edward III and so came to the notice of another of those sons – the great John of Gaunt, Duke of Lancaster, a connection of whom he later married. He was taken into the service of the king and travelled widely abroad, becoming fluent in Latin, French and Italian and an expert in medieval science. He was made a justice of the peace, entered parliament, and held various important posts in connection with the customs. For the offspring of a family of vintners, Chaucer had climbed very high.

John Gower, who was born about 1330 and died in 1407, appears also to have been acceptable in Court circles: he was descended from a family of Kentish gentlemen and became the owner of fairly extensive lands in East Anglia. Beyond this, little is known of him.

William Langland is a shadowy figure as compared with the two others, for he is known only from the lines of *Piers Plowman*. He appears to have been born in Shropshire and educated in the Benedictine priory at Great Malvern, and to have lived for some time in London – though at a very much humbler social level than either of his contemporaries.

Separate from these, both in time and character, are the Norfolk Pastons, three generations of whom present themselves in their letters, which were written between 1440 and 1486. As owners of widely scattered properties, they are constantly worried about how to keep them intact in the period of near-anarchy before and during the Wars of the Roses. Quite unreflecting about the deeper causes of their troubles, their warnings and encouragements to each other pass to and fro like the flight of bats in the twilight – and with as little influence on great affairs.

One important feature common to all these writers is that they use English: Chaucer's *Canterbury Tales*, Langland's *Piers Plowman*, Gower's *Confessio Amantis*, and the letters of the Pastons are among the earliest specimens still surviving. It has already been remarked as one of the results of the Norman Conquest that the Old English speech went underground, submerged by the Norman-French of the conquerors. Yet it did not die: it remained the language of the poor and even continued some sort of a written existence, though deeply modified in both its written and spoken forms by the invaders' tongue. Somewhere in the first half of the fourteenth century, when Englishmen first began to look upon the French as foreigners and challenged them in the Hundred Years War, the English language was taken up again by the educated classes and became a serviceable instrument for poetry or prose.

Something of a half-way stage can be seen in Gower, who wrote his three major works in English, Latin and French respectively, as though he was not quite certain which to use. His *Confessio Amantis* ('The Lover's Shrift') in spite of its Latin title is written deliberately in the native tongue of the land:

> *And furthermore, since few men write*
> *In our English, I think to make*
> *One book at least for England's sake.*

Yet the English of this time is still far from the present-day form and most people can only read it easily in a modernized version. Look, for instance, at this extract from a Paston letter in the original spelling:

> Ryth reverend and worchepfull modyr, I recomand me on to you as humbylly as I can thynk, desyiring most hertly to her of your welfare and hertes ese, whyche I pray god send yow as hastyly as eny hert can thynk.[1]

As the Paston letters go, this is a straightforward passage; yet it

---

[1] 'Right reverend and worshipful mother, I recommend me unto you as humbly as I can think, desiring most heartily to hear of your welfare and heart's ease, which I pray God send you as hastily as any heart can think.'

shows that English did not spring upon the world fully formed but grew naturally from awkwardness into maturity.

William Langland in his prologue to *Piers Plowman* tells of a dream he had, when he fell asleep while resting on the Malvern Hills – and it may serve as our prologue too:

> I dreamt a marvellous dream: I was in a wilderness, I could not tell where, and looking eastwards I saw a tower high up against the sun, and splendidly built on top of a hill; and far beneath it was a great gulf . . . dreadful to see. But between the tower and the gulf I saw a smooth plain, thronged with all kinds of people, high and low together, moving busily about their worldly affairs.

In this 'smooth plain,' which was Langland's world, we too may discern our informants: Langland himself, in what he described as his 'shaggy woollen clothes'; Chaucer the courtier; the love-stricken Gower; and the careful, legal-minded Pastons. What have they to tell us about the matters with which this book deals?

Life on the Land

First, about the land as it was in the later Middle Ages. It is evident that the rigid manorial system now lies near to death and that wages rather than unpaid labour services govern the relationship between lord and villein. Thus Langland, in his allegorical style, speaks of Truth as the lord whom all men should serve and who pays his villeins well:

> 'By St Peter!', said a ploughman, pushing his way through the crowd, 'I know Him . . . Conscience and Commonsense showed me the way to His place, and they made me swear to serve Him for ever, and do His sowing and planting for as long as I can work. I've been His man for the last fifty years; I've sown His seed and herded His beasts, and looked after all His affairs, indoors and out. I ditch and dig, sow and thresh, and do whatever Truth tells me – tailoring and tinkering, spinning and weaving – I put my hand to anything He bids me. And Truth is pleased with my work . . . He pays me well, and sometimes gives

me extra; for He's as ready with His wages as any poor man could wish, and never fails to pay His men each night.'

But Langland is also familiar with free men (free at least in practice) who were able to carry their labour about with them and in a modern way look for jobs on the land. He describes the voice of Reason speaking to him 'one hot harvest time':

'Why can't you . . . rake the corn for the harvesters, or help them mow and stack it, or bind up the sheaves? Or why don't you get up early and join the reapers, or find yourself a job as a head-reaper or a hayward, and stand with a horn in your hand, and sleep out at night to guard the corn in my fields from thieves and pilferers? Or why couldn't you cobble shoes, or watch the sheep and the pigs, or get some hedging and harrowing done, or drive the hogs and geese to market? At all events you ought to do *something* that's useful to the community. . . .'

The later Middle Ages was a time both of labour shortage and of the weakening of the bonds that tied men to their lords – a time of opportunity when men could do well for themselves. An ambitious manor reeve, as we have seen,[1] was especially well-placed to take advantage of the new conditions. Chaucer describes such a man efficiently controlling the manor, no longer on an annual but a permanent basis, and in the process rising clear above the villein class:

> *He kept his bins and garners very trim;*
> *No auditor could gain a point on him.*
> *And he could judge by watching drought and rain*
> *The yield he might expect from seed and grain.*
> *His master's sheep, his animals and hens,*
> *Pigs, horses, dairies, stores and cattle-pens*
> *Were wholly trusted to his government.*
> *And he was under contract to present*
> *The accounts, right from his master's earliest years.*
> *No one had ever caught him in arrears.*
> *No bailiff, serf or herdsman dared to kick,*
> *He knew their dodges, knew their every trick. . . .*

[1] See p. 162

> *He had grown rich and had a store of treasure*
> *Well tucked away, yet out it came to pleasure*
> *His lord with subtle loans or gifts of goods,*
> *To earn his thanks and even coats and hoods.*

Chaucer also gives us a memorable picture of a prosperous franklin – one whose father, probably, had risen out of the ranks of the peasantry to become a substantial yeoman, so that the son inherited both land and wealth and acquired position too, as justice of the peace and member of parliament. This was the type of family from which many of the Tudor nobility were later to be drawn.

> *His bread, his ale were finest of the fine*
> *And no-one had a better stock of wine.*
> *His house was never short of bake-meat pies,*
> *Of fish and flesh, and these in such supplies*
> *It positively snowed with meat and drink*
> *And all the dainties that a man could think....*
> *As Justice at the Sessions none stood higher;*
> *He often had been Member for the Shire....*
> *He was a model among landed gentry.*

But what about the Black Death, which so upset the relationship between men and the land? Even though the Pastons lived much later, Chaucer was nine at its first savage outbreak and Gower and Langland both about twenty, so that all three must have remembered it. But here our authors almost fall silent – perhaps because plague was a continuing threat, to be feared and if possible forgotten. Chaucer, however, in 'The Pardoner's Tale' speaks of three rioters,

> *Who long before the morning service bell*
> *Were sitting in a tavern for a drink.*
> *And as they sat, they heard the hand-bell clink*
> *Before a coffin going to the grave.*

On asking a child about the corpse, they hear that he had been struck down by 'a privy thief, they call him Death' who 'killed a thousand in the present plague'.

> *The publican joined in with, 'By St. Mary,*
> *What the child says is right; you'd best be wary,*
> *This very year he killed, in a large village*
> *A mile away, man, woman, serf at tillage,*
> *Page in the household, children – all there were.'*

Langland may be allowed to close the matter with his wry comment on the impartiality of death: 'It is very hard to tell a knight from a serf when he comes to lie in the church vaults.'

Commerce and Industry

We may direct our attention next to the world of trade. Each of our literary sources is well aware both of the wealth to be gained there and of the sharp practice that often accompanied its acquisition. Indeed, the puritanically-minded Langland can only look upon the riches of merchants as evidence of their corruptness, with town authorities helping them to defraud their poorer neighbours:

> They grow rich by selling at retail prices, and invest in properties as robbers of the bellies of the poor. For how could they build themselves such tall houses and buy up lands and tenements, if they were honest dealers? But Lucre has begged the Mayor to accept money from them ... to let them stay in business undisturbed.

It was not so much corruption as the greater availability of money and especially of credit that characterized the increased trading activity of the later Middle Ages. 'We merchants use our money like a plough; we can get credit while our name will run,' says the merchant in Chaucer's 'Shipman's Tale', which also gives a clear outline of how money was lent. A loan was negotiated for a definite term and a date fixed for its repayment; for a small sum passing between friends, a word might clinch the deal. But the Pastons still used tally-sticks on occasion: one of the letters records 'a tally with my cousin Fenn of 500 marks and more, for to be changed upon such places as a man might have most speedy payment.' In large transactions, however, the borrower often signed a bond, which he recovered when he paid his debt. This was what Chaucer's merchant did as regards a sum of 20,000 crowns:

> *The bond that he had signed became his own,*
> *For he paid down the money to a franc*
> *To certain Lombards at their Paris bank.*

All this sounds eminently respectable – a necessary part of a trader's life. It takes Langland, with his distrust of all but the very simplest business activity, to suggest other possibilities:

> I did pick up a thing or two, chiefly from Jews and Lombards. They showed me how to weigh coins with a balance, clip the heavier ones, and then lend them out, all for love of the cross – the one on the back of the gold pieces!

But such swindles were not restricted to alien tradesmen. Chaucer's miller exclaims:

> *The more they try to do me in the deal,*
> *When the time comes the more I mean to steal.*
> *Instead of flour they shall be given bran.*

And Langland tells of a man who 'went to school with the drapers, and was shown how to stretch the selvedge and make the cloth look longer . . . till ten or eleven yards were stretched into thirteen'. Likewise of a woollen weaver who 'employed spinners to spin it out for her and paid them by the pound, but . . . the pound weight weighed a quarter more' than it should.

In spite of such devious practices, the woollen industry was by this time clearly pre-eminent. Thus the pious Langland finds it natural to compare the processes involved in cloth-finishing with those of a more heavenly manufacture:

> Before newly-woven cloth is fit to wear, it has to be cleaned in fulling-mills or trodden underfoot in water; and it does not come to the tailor until it is combed with teasels, fluffed out and thoroughly stretched. So also a new-born child, until it is christened in the name of Christ and confirmed by the bishop, is still a heathen.

Criticism of the Church

This brings us to the Church, against which all three poets let loose a flood of criticism. Not so the Pastons, however, who refer only incidentally to the daily round of the Church's life as it touches their own. They date their letters by Church festivals— Trinity Sunday, the 'Wednesday next before Palm Sunday', St Katherine's Day – and close them with prayers for divine protection. When John Paston falls ill, his wife sends an image of wax of his exact weight to the miracle-working shrine of Our Lady of Walsingham. The Pastons in fact were like most men of their time in speaking the language of religion. The poets speak it, too: the difference is that they use it to ask questions and to make protests.

One of the most general criticisms was that the Church had lost her original purity – a fact which could be clearly seen in the lives of her clergy from the Pope himself downwards. Let John Gower speak first:

> Lo now, consider and behold
> The life of clerks in days of old.
> I have heard said that they were then
> The guide and pattern of all men ...
> Then Holy Church was liberal
> And gave and did great alms to all
> Poor men, or such as stood in need.
> The clerks were chaste in word and deed,
> A model for their flocks to heed ...
> Thus was the ship of Peter steered
> By those who were its masters then ...
>
> But many clerks are to be found
> So worldly-minded, they are glad
> When holy orders may be had –
> Not for the virtues of that state,
> But only to grow rich and great
> And be for ever clear of need.
> And thus, by pomp and petty greed,

> *Up grow the Scribe and Pharisee*
> *To Moses' or to Peter's See,*
> *And sit aloft in that high chair,*
> *And often damage, being there,*
> *The faith entrusted to their keeping –*
> *For Christ's cause finds them all day sleeping.*

And Langland is making the same point when he looks back longingly to the early days of the Church, when the saints were so close to God that they were at one with nature too:

> And every lion and leopard that stalked the forests, the bears and the wild boars and all the other beasts, would fall at those hermits' feet and caress them with their tails. ... For they showed them all the gentleness that animals know, and as they roamed the forests they would stop to lick the saints' hands and crouch down before them.

For, a little later, Langland underlines the contrast with his own day in the question 'To what then shall I compare you wealthy clergymen?' – words which seem to echo the protests of John Wyclif and the Lollards.

Chaucer does not criticize the Church so outspokenly as Gower, but all through the *Canterbury Tales* – and especially, perhaps, in his famous description of the Nun – a picture is drawn of an institution whose spirit needs renewal. Consider this nun – a prioress, in fact. She is well mannered:

> *At meat her manners were well-taught withal;*
> *No morsel from her lips did she let fall,*
> *Nor dipped her fingers in the sauce too deep;*
> *But she could carry a morsel up and keep*
> *The smallest drop from falling on her breast.*

She has the social graces:

> *Pleasant and friendly in her ways, and straining*
> *To counterfeit a courtly kind of grace,*
> *A stately bearing fitting to her place,*
> *And to seem dignified in all her dealings.*

She has charity, too, in small matters.:

> *She was so charitably solicitous*
> *She used to weep if she but saw a mouse*
> *Caught in a trap, if it were dead or bleeding,*

She is the possessor of elegant jewellery:

> *Her cloak, I noticed, had a graceful charm.*
> *She wore a coral trinket on her arm,*
> *A set of beads, the gaudies tricked in green,*
> *Whence hung a golden brooch of brightest sheen*
> *On which there first was graven a crowned 'A'.*
> *And lower, 'Amor vincit omnia'.*

One cannot avoid the feeling, however, that no lion would lick her hands or crouch down before her.

Langland strikes exactly the same note, though – as is his fashion – more explicitly:

> For it is quite the thing nowadays for Father John and Monsignor Geoffrey to wear silver girdles and carry daggers and sheath-knives studded with gilt. And as for their Breviaries, the weapons they should use for saying the Office, they wait for someone to offer them silver before they would dream of using them.

It was easy to spot the disease – far less so to find its cause; in any case, to look for causes as modern historians do was not the medieval way. Nevertheless, Langland indicated that some of the Church's ills could be traced to the quality of its clergy. Both bishops and priests were ignorant men, many of whom had bought their way to promotion – the evil of simony: 'Even Popes now are appointing the sons of simony to keep God's sanctuary.' Some bishops, therefore, were 'men who could scarcely read':

> And the same is true of priests who have neither learning nor honest blood . . . I wonder that the Bishop ordains such priests to betray ignorant layfolk who know no better.

Some of the trouble, in Langland's view, was directly social.

Priests, and bishops too, have not 'honest blood' – they come from the wrong class:

> A cleric's duty is to serve Christ, and leave carting and labouring to ignorant serfs. And no-one should take Holy Orders unless he comes from a family of freemen . . . Serfs and beggars' children should toil with their hands, while men of noble blood should serve God and their fellow men as befits their rank . . . But nowadays bondmen's children are made into bishops.

But Langland pictures the Church as betrayed above all by its love of money. He describes Lady Lucre whispering to a friar in the confessional:

> I will roof your church, build you a cloister, whitewash your walls, glaze your windows, have paintings and images made, and pay for everything. People will be saying I am a lay sister of your Order.

The Weakness of the Law

This dissatisfaction with the standards of the Church, leading to a call for practical improvements, is to some extent paralleled by discontent with the law. The one had lost its purity, the other its impartiality. Gower expresses this clearly:

> *The law is doubled-faced, therefore*
> *All justice now has lost its way*
> *And righteousness is gone astray.*
> *And thus on all sides is revealed*
> *The ulcer which is never healed*
> *And which is borne by everyone.*

However, the fault lay, not in the actual machinery of the law, which was soundly constructed, but in the way in which the machine had come to be worked. Locked in a disastrously long struggle with France, the English monarchy had sacrificed more and more of its authority to the barons in return for supplies of money and men. The barons raised what were really private armies, whose members wore such badges as Warwick the King-maker's bear and ragged staff; when the Hundred Years War came at last to an end, they were readily available to fight at home. The power of the law could then be freely abused by powerful interests, backed by main force. *The Paston Letters* shows the kind of thing that happened.

In the first place, the tenure of property became very insecure. A certain friar, for example, laid claim to one of the manors held by the Pastons:

> This day at ten of the clock Edmund Paston and the parson of Oxnead went out of the manor down to the Wantown Gap, for they heard tidings that the friar was coming ... And he came riding from the Wantown Gap to the great gate; and there he lighted and knocked on the gate ... And then came on Edmund Paston and the parson, and asked him what was the cause of his coming at this time. And he said, for to enter in the manor of Oxnead, the which his father was possessed of ... And even forthwith he pressed to the gateward to have laid hand on the gate. And then the said Edmund put him from the gate and said ... 'an' thou layest any hand on the gate I shall see thy heart bleed or thou mine.' And then [the friar] stooped down and took up earth and delivered to his man, saying to them that came with him: 'I charge you all on the King's behalf ye bear record that I take here possession of mine inheritance'.

And in such an anarchic world small men would creep in under the shadow of big ones, entering their service and gaining both their protection when their rights were attacked and support for their own aggressions. This the claimant of the Paston manor was quick to do:

> [The friar] said plainly in this town that he shall have Oxnead, and that he have my lord of Suffolk's good lordship, and he will be his good lord in that matter.

But when one of the great lords themselves was out to seize land, there were no half-measures and no attempt to gain even the colour of the law. The Pastons were unlucky because, as well as having to deal with the friar at Oxnead, they had to face the Lord

Moleyns in their manor at Gresham. In a petition to the king, John Paston states how the baron asserted his claim:

> The said lord sent to the said mansion a riotous people, to the number of one thousand persons ... arrayed in manner of war with ... guns, pans with fire ... long poles to draw down houses, ladders, picks with which they mined down the walls, and long trees with which they broke up gates and doors, and so came into the said mansion ...

So much for the insecurity of property. But security of person and even of life was also endangered in these lawless days. A certain John Northwood, in a letter included among the Paston collection, tells how Sir Humphrey Stafford riding one night was passed by a Sir Robert Harcourt coming the other way. Behind Sir Humphrey rode his son Richard:

> And Sir Robert smote him [Richard] a great stroke on the head with his sword, and Richard with his dagger hastily went toward him. And as he stumbled, one of Harcourt's men smote him in the back with a knife. His father heard noise and rode towards them ... and in the going down off his horse one smote him on the head with an edged weapon, that he fell down, and his son fell down before him as good as dead. And all this was done, as men say, in a Paternoster while.

Thirdly, there was corruption of juries (and of witnesses too) even by the legal officers themselves and sometimes at the king's command – open as he was to the pressures of great men. So Lord Moleyns made headway in the courts, in spite of his open disregard of the law in respect of the Paston manor at Gresham:

> Also the sheriff informed us that he hath writing from the king that he shall make such a panel to acquit the Lord Moleyns. And also ... as far as we can conceive and feel, the sheriff will panel gentlemen to acquit the lord, and jurors to acquit his men.

Thus the weakness of the Crown enabled the barons systematically to pervert the law. Offences against the king's peace were often formally condoned, as appears for instance in *The Paston*

Letters account of the duke of Suffolk, of whose capacity for 'great heaving and shoving' their authors were painfully aware:

> The Duke of Suffolk is pardoned, and hath his men waiting upon him, and is right well at ease and merry, and is in the King's good grace, and in the good conceit of all the lords, as well as ever he was.

But not for long, in this age of violence. In 1450 the duke was murdered off Dover on his way to exile, a couple of months before Cade's rebellion, when the men of Kent vainly demonstrated in London against the chronic misgovernment of the realm. Instead, the end of the Hundred Years War in 1453 ushered in the Wars of the Roses, fought between rival groups of ambitious nobles and their bands of indentured retainers – many of them, as we have already noticed, soldiers returning from the continent.

Henry VI – who was mentally afflicted in his later years but resolutely supported by his French queen, Margaret of Anjou – derived his claim to the throne from the deposition of Richard II in 1399 by his grandfather, Henry IV, the first king of the House of Lancaster. Possession was now contested by a rival line of descendants of Edward III, the House of York, whose head in 1461 fought his way to the throne as Edward IV, helped by Warwick the King-maker. Eight years later the earl changed sides. A second round of small-scale battles then secured a six months' 'readoption' of King Henry before the final Yorkist victories at Barnet – where two of the Pastons fought on the losing side – and Tewkesbury resulted in the deaths of Warwick, of Henry's only son, and of Henry himself, a hapless prisoner in the Tower. The Yorkist régime then continued under Edward IV, his young son Edward V, and the presumed murderer of the latter, his uncle, who became Richard III and fell before the reviving Lancastrian power at Bosworth.

The fifteenth century was not, however, all violence. Perpendicular architecture, for example, was then in its prime, seen to perfection in such splendid structures as King's College chapel, Cambridge, with its glorious fan-vaulting and huge rectangular-framed expanses of glass, but also in the great church towers which adorn so many East Anglian and Somerset villages. Henry VI, the founder of Eton and King's, continued the stimulus to education given at the close of the preceding century by William of Wykeham's foundations at Winchester and New College, Oxford. His Yorkist rival, the usurper Edward IV, was the patron of Caxton's first English printing press at Westminster. The towns as a whole suffered hardly at all in the Wars of the Roses, deadly as they were to the rival royal houses and the baronial families who espoused their cause.

Yet, when the little armies of baronial retainers had fought their last battle on Bosworth Field in 1485, the medieval society which we have tried to picture in this book, with all its faults and merits, was already giving place to new groupings of men. The peoples of Britain were stepping unawares across the threshold of another age.

APPENDIX I

Dates of Main Events Mentioned in the Text
(Foreign events italicized)

B.C.

- *c.* 5500 Britain became an island
- *c.* 3200 First Neolithic settlements in Britain
- *c.* 3000 *Urban civilizations already flourishing in the Middle East*
- *c.* 2000 *Bronze Age civilization of Crete and eastern Mediterranean*
- *c.* 1900 Use of bronze began to affect Britain
- *c.* 1500 Completion of Stonehenge in its later form
- *c.* 600 First large immigration of Celts, bringing Hallstatt Iron Age culture
- *c.* 400 Second Celtic immigration, bringing La Tène culture
- *c.* 325 Visit of Pytheas
- *c.* 100 Belgic immigration
- 55, 54 Landings of Julius Caesar

A.D.

- 43 Roman conquest begun
- 61 Revolt of Boudicca
- 84 Agricola's victory at Mons Graupius
- *c.* 133 Completion of Hadrian's Wall
- *c.* 143 Antonine Wall built
- *c.* 280 Forts of the Saxon Shore constructed
- 314 *Church Council of Arles held under Constantine's patronage*
- 367 Concerted attack on Britain of Saxons, Picts, and Scots
- 410 Letter of emperor Honorius to native authorities in Britain *Rome sacked by the Goths*
- *c.* 450 Jutish settlements in Kent
- 461 Death of St Patrick
- *c.* 500 British victory at Mons Badonicus
- 563–597 Columba at Iona
- 597 Landing of Augustine in Kent
- 632 Edwin, first Christian king of Northumbria, killed (at Hatfield)
- 635 Aidan's mission entered Northumbria
- 663 Synod of Whitby
- 669–690 Theodore archbishop of Canterbury
- 685 Victory of Picts at Nechtansmere

196

687 Death of St Cuthbert
731 Bede's Ecclesiastical History completed
757–796 Reign of Offa the Great of Mercia
793 Viking raid on Lindisfarne
800 *Charlemagne crowned emperor at Rome*
825 Egbert of Wessex defeated the Mercians (at Ellendun)
838 Final absorption of Cornwall in England
843 Kenneth Macalpin king of Scots (of Alba)
865 Danish army of conquest landed in East Anglia
871–899 Alfred the Great king of Wessex
886 London recaptured from the Danes
c. 910–c. 950 Howell the Good 'King of all the Welsh'
c. 910 *Abbey of Cluny founded*
911–954 Reconquest of the Danelaw
911 *Duchy of Normandy established by Northmen*
960–988 Dunstan archbishop of Canterbury
973 Edgar crowned at Bath and accepted as suzerain in Britain
c. 973 Lothian ceded to Scotland
1016–1035 Cnut king of all England
1034 Duncan king of Scotland (including Cumbria and Strathclyde)
1042–1066 Reign of Edward the Confessor
1066–1087 Reign of William the Conqueror
1078 Keep of the Tower of London (White Tower) begun
1086 Domesday Book survey made
1087–1100 Reign of William II
1093–1109 Anselm archbishop of Canterbury
1095 *First Crusade proclaimed by the pope*
1098 *Abbey of Cîteaux founded*
1100–1135 Reign of Henry I
1118 First Cistercian monastery in England (Waverley)
1124–1153 David I king of Scotland
1135–1154 Reign of Stephen
1138 Battle of the Standard
1147–1148 *Second Crusade*
c. 1150 *Rise of the universities of Bologna and Paris*
1154–1189 Reign of Henry II
1162–1170 Thomas Becket archbishop of Canterbury
1174 Gothic architecture at Canterbury
1181 Assize of Arms
1189–1199 Reign of Richard I
1189–1192 *Third Crusade*
1199–1216 Reign of John
1204 *Normandy annexed to the French Crown*
1209 *Franciscan Order founded*
1215 Magna Carta
1216–1272 Reign of Henry III

c. 1250 *Rise of the Hanseatic League*
1263 Western Isles annexed to Scotland (Battle of Largs)
1265 Burgesses summoned to a 'parliament' by Simon de Montfort
1272–1307 Reign of Edward I
1277 Conquest of Wales begun
1282 Death of Llywelyn, Prince of Wales
1286–1371 Scottish Wars of Independence
1290 Expulsion of the Jews from England
1298 Battle of Falkirk
1307–1327 Reign of Edward II
1314 Battle of Bannockburn
1327–1377 Reign of Edward III
1329–1371 David II king of Scotland
1333 Battle of Halidon Hill
1337 Outbreak of the Hundred Years War
1346 *Battle of Crécy*
1346 Battle of Neville's Cross
1347 *Capture of Calais*
1348–1349 Black Death
1351 Statute of Labourers
1356 *Battle of Poitiers*
1358 *Jacquerie (peasant revolt) in France*
1363 *Wool staple first located at Calais*
1377–1399 Reign of Richard II
1379, 1382 Foundation of New College, Oxford, and Winchester College
(by William of Wykeham)
1381 Peasants' Revolt
1384 Death of Wyclif
1399–1413 Reign of Henry IV
1400 Death of Chaucer
1413–1422 Reign of Henry V
1415 *Battle of Agincourt*
1422–1461 Reign of Henry VI
1440, 1441 Henry VI's foundations at Cambridge and Eton
c. 1450 *Printing established on the continent (Gutenberg Bible, 1456)*
1450 Jack Cade's Revolt
1453 *End of Hundred Years War*
1459–61, 1469–71 Main campaigns of Wars of the Roses
1461–1485 Reigns of Yorkist kings (Edward IV, Edward V, Richard III)
1468–1469 Orkney and Shetland pledged from Norway to Scotland
1477 Caxton's printing press set up at Westminster
1485 Battle of Bosworth Field

APPENDIX II

References for Source Quotations

Chapter 3

p. 30 BEDE: *Ecclesiastical History of the English Nation,* Book I, c. xv (Everyman edition, p. 23).

p. 35 Early English poem, *The Wanderer* (*English Historical Documents,* general editor, D. C. Douglas, Vol. I, pp. 801–3).

p. 41 Early Welsh poem, *The Misfortunes of Princess Heledd* (broadcast translation by Professor T. J. Morgan, quoted in N. K. Chadwick, *Celtic Britain,* p. 108).

Chapter 4

p. 44 BEDE's *Ecclesiastical History,* Book II, c. xiii (Everyman, p. 91).

p. 47 BEDE's *Ecclesiastical History,* Book II, c. xvi (Everyman, p. 95).

p. 54 *The Anglo-Saxon Chronicle,* A.D. 681 (Everyman edition, p. 44).

Chapter 5

p. 56 Letter to Ethelred, King of Northumbria (*English Historical Documents,* Vol. I, p. 776).

p. 58 Torbjorn Hornklove, poem on Hafrsfiord (quoted in R. H. Hodgkin, *History of the Anglo-Saxons,* Vol. II, p. 690).

p. 65 Grant of land to York Minster (*English Historical Documents,* Vol. I, p. 506).

p. 65 Alfred's version of St Augustine's Soliloquies (quoted in Hodgkin, Vol. II, p. 680).

p. 66 Alfred's version of St Augustine's Soliloquies (*English Historical Documents,* Vol. I, p. 844).

p. 68 Early English poem on the battle of Maldon (*English Historical Documents,* Vol. I, p. 297).

Chapter 6

p. 81 RICHARD FITZ NIGEL, *Dialogus de Scaccario* (translation by C. Johnson, Nelson's Medieval Classics, p. 60).

Chapter 7

p. 97 AELFRIC, *Colloquies* (*They Saw It Happen, 55 B.C.–A.D. 1485,* edited by W. O. Hassall, p. 26).

Chapter 9

p. 119 *Materials for the History of Thomas Becket* (Rolls Series, edited by J. G. Robertson, Vol. II, p. 15; *English Historical Documents*, Vol. II, p. 768).

p. 121 WALTER DANIEL: *Life of Ailred of Rievaulx* (translation by F. M. Powicke, Nelson's Medieval Classics, p. 30).

Chapter 10

p. 134 quoted by F. POLLOCK and F. W. MAITLAND, *History of English Law Before the Time of Edward I*, p. 233.

p. 138 BARTHOLOMEW DE COTTON: *Historia Anglicana* (Rolls Series, edited by H. R. Luard, p. 166).

p. 139 quoted by G. S. BARROW, *Feudal Britain*, p. 144.

Chapter 11

p. 142 JEAN FROISSART: *Chronicle*, first translated by Lord Berners, vi, p. 1.

p. 143 FROISSART'S *Chronicle*, vi, 210, 129–30.

p. 144 FROISSART'S *Chronicle*, vi, 310.

p. 150 FROISSART'S *Chronicle*, xvii (*Source Book of Scottish History*, edited by W. C. Dickinson and others, Vol. I, p. 204).

p. 152 Constable's inventory, 22 October, translated by J. Stevenson: *Documents Illustrative of the History of Scotland*, Vol. II, pp. 322–3 (quoted in *They Saw It Happen*, p. 135).

Chapter 12

p. 155 WALTER OF HENLEY: *Husbandry*, 11 (thirteenth century writer edited by E. Lamond).

p. 156 ROBERT OF AVESBURY: *De gestis mirabilibus regis Edwardi tertii* (Rolls Series, edited by E. M. Thompson, p. 407).

p. 158 Stonor papers, first published in *They Saw It Happen*, p. 158.

p. 159 JOHN GOWER: *Mirour de l'Omme* (translated by G. C. Coulton, *Social Life in Britain from the Conquest to the Reformation*, p. 353).

p. 160 Holkham papers, first published in *They Saw It Happen*, pp. 162–3.

p. 163 FROISSART'S *Chronicle*, c. ccclxxxi.

p. 163 THOMAS WALSINGHAM: *Historia Anglicana* (Rolls Series, edited by H. T. Riley, Vol. II, p. 9).

p. 163 FROISSART'S *Chronicle*, c. ccclxxxi.

p. 166 JOHN FORDUN: *Chronicles of the People of Scotland* (*Source Book of Scottish History*, Vol. I, p. 104).

Chapter 13

p. 175 *Fleta*, Latin tract quoted in *They Saw It Happen*, p. 127.

p. 177 SIR THOMAS SMITH, *De Republica Anglorum*, edited by L. Alston, p. 137 (quoted in E. Lipson, *Economic History of England*, Vol. I, p. 312)

p. 178 quoted by A. FRANKLIN: *Seven Miracle Plays*, p. 19.

p. 179 see Penguin Classics version by J. F. GOODRIDGE, p. 298.

Chapter 14

p. 180 *Confessio Amantis*, lines 25–31.

p. 182 ibid. 22–4.

p. 182 *The Paston Letters* (Everyman edition, Vol. II, p. 151).

p. 183 *Piers the Ploughman* (Penguin Classics edition, p. 63).

p. 183 ibid., p. 116.

p. 184 ibid., p. 295.

p. 184 *Canterbury Tales* (Penguin Classics edition, p. 35 – Prologue).

p. 185 ibid., p. 28.

p. 185 ibid., p. 268 (Pardoner's Tale).

p. 186 *Piers the Ploughman*, p. 85.

p. 187 *Canterbury Tales*, p. 183 (Shipman's Tale).

p. 187 *Piers the Ploughman*, p. 111.

p. 187 *Canterbury Tales*, p. 128 (Reeve's Tale).

p. 187 *Piers the Ploughman*, p. 105.

p. 187 ibid., p. 230.

p. 188 *Confessio Amantis*, lines 193–217.

p. 189 *Piers the Ploughman,* p. 222.

p. 189 *Canterbury Tales*, p. 22 (Prologue).

p. 190 *Piers the Ploughman*, p. 220.

p. 190 ibid., p. 174.

p. 191 ibid., p. 296.

p. 191 ibid., p. 84.

p. 191 *Confessio Amantis*, lines 130–5.

p. 192 *Paston Letters*, Vol. I, p. 6.

p. 192 ibid., p. 22.

p. 193 ibid., p. 32.

p. 193 ibid., p. 16.

p. 194 ibid., p. 38.

APPENDIX III

Book List

1. THE EARLIEST INHABITANTS

Introductory

C. H. B. and M. QUENNELL, *Everyday Life in Prehistoric Times* (Batsford).

Authorities

J. and C. HAWKES, *Prehistoric Britain* (Penguin Books).

V. G. CHILDE, *The Prehistoric Communities of the British Isles* (Chambers).

S. THOMAS, *Pre-Roman Britain* (Studio Vista) – a full and varied collection of plates, with brief introduction.

2. ROMAN BRITAIN

Introductory

A. FOX and A. SORRELL, *Roman Britain* (Lutterworth).

Authorities

I. A. RICHMOND, *Roman Britain* (Penguin Books).

A. L. F. RIVET, *Town and Country in Roman Britain* (Hutchinson's U.L.)

C. G. BOON, *Roman Silchester* (Parrish).

A. BIRLEY, *Life in Roman Britain* (Batsford).

3. THE COMING OF THE ENGLISH

Introductory

R. R. SELLMAN, *The Anglo-Saxons* (Methuen).

Authorities

R. H. HODGKIN, *A History of the Anglo-Saxons* (O.U.P.): cc. III–VII – a classic work, beautifully illustrated.

N. K. CHADWICK, *Celtic Britain* (Thames and Hudson); cc. II–IV – an enthusiastic account of the kingdoms which resisted the English invasion.

P. H. BLAIR, *Roman Britain and Early England* (Nelson): pp. 149–92.

4. THE CONVERSION OF ENGLAND

Introductory

B. E. DODD and T. C. HERITAGE, *The Early Christians in Britain* (Longmans): cc. II–IV.

Authorities

J. GODFREY, *The Church in Anglo-Saxon England* (C.U.P.): cc. V–IX – a full, up-to-date survey.

HODGKIN, op. cit: cc. VIII and IX.

D. WHITELOCK, *The Beginnings of English Society* (Penguin Books): c. VIII.

5. THE IMPACT OF SCANDINAVIA

Introductory

C. OMAN, *Alfred, King of the English* (Dent).

Authorities

T. D. KENDRICK, *A History of the Vikings* (Methuen).

H. R. LOYN, *Anglo-Saxon England and the Norman Conquest* (Longmans): pp. 49–62.

W. C. DICKINSON, *Scotland from the Earliest Times to 1603* (Nelson): c. IV.

6. THE FRANCO-NORMAN CONQUEST

Introductory

R. R. SELLMAN, *Norman England* (Methuen).

Authorities

F. M. STENTON. *Anglo-Saxon England* (O.U.P.): cc. XVI and XVII.

R. BARLOW, *The Feudal Kingdom of England* (Longmans): cc. 2–4.

C. BROOKE, *From Alfred to Henry III* (Nelson): cc. 5 and 6.

7. LIFE ON THE MANOR

Introductory

C. H. B. and M. QUENNELL, *A History of Everyday Things in England, Book 1* (Batsford): pp. 65–71 on agriculture and pp. 119–23 on manor houses.

Authorities

J. H. CLAPHAM, *Concise Economic History of Britain to 1750* (C.U.P.): pp. 77–116.

H. S. BENNETT, *Life on the English Manor* (C.U.P.): cc. II–VIII.

D. M. STENTON, *English Society in the Early Middle Ages* (Penguin Books).

O. G. TOMKEIEFF, *Life in Norman England* (Batsford): c. III.

8. THE GROWTH OF TRADE AND TOWNS

Introductory

T. K. DERRY, *A Short Economic History of Britain* (O.U.P.): pp. 38–53.

Authorities

A. L. POOLE, *From Domesday Book to Magna Carta* (O.U.P.): c. III.

A. L. POOLE, (editor), *Medieval England* (O.U.P.): c. VII – by E. M. Carus-Wilson.

R. J. MITCHELL, and M. R. D. LEYS, *A History of London Life* (Penguin Books): c. I.

J. J. BAGLEY, *Life in Medieval England* (Batsford): c. III.

O. G. TOMKEIEFF, op. cit. : c. IV.

9. THE BUILDINGS AND WORK OF THE CHURCH

Introductory

L. E. ELLIOTT-BINNS, *The Story of the English Church* (S.P.C.K.): c. 3.

Authorities

Medieval England: c. XII – by D. Knowles and c. XIII – by G. F. Webb.

J. R. H. MOORMAN, *Church Life in England in the Thirteenth Century* (C.U.P.).

C. BROOKE, op. cit: c. 8.

10. THE MAKING OF THE LAW

Introductory

W. E. TATE and C. H. C. BLOUNT, *Government in England* (O.U.P.).

Authorities

J. E. A. JOLLIFFE, *The Constitutional History of Medieval England* (Black).

F. W. MAITLAND, *The Constitutional History of England* (C.U.P.): Period I, especially section A – sixty-year-old lectures by the greatest of legal historians.

G. HOLMES, *The Later Middle Ages* (Nelson): c. 4.

11. WARS AND WARFARE

Introductory

R. R. SELLMAN, *Castles and Fortresses* (Methuen).

R. R. SELLMAN, *Medieval English Warfare* (Methuen).

Authorities

Medieval England: c. III – by A. J. Taylor and c. IV – by R. C. Smail.

B. M. ST J. O'NEILL, *Castles* (H.M.S.O.) – an introduction to the series of guides issued for castles controlled by the Ministry of Works.

C. W. C. OMAN, *A History of the Art of War in the Middle Ages* (Methuen).

12. THE CHANGING VILLAGE

Introductory

DERRY, op. cit.: c. V.

Authorities

M. MCKISACK, *The Fourteenth Century* (O.U.P.): c. XI.

CLAPHAM, op. cit.: pp. 110–24.

HOLMES, op. cit.: pp. 136–48.

13. CRAFTS AND CRAFTSMEN

Introductory

G. SCOTT THOMSON, *Wool Merchants of the Fifteenth Century* (Longmans).

Authorities

MCKISACK, op. cit.: c. XII.

E. F. JACOB, *The Fifteenth Century* (O.U.P.): c. VIII (c).

E. POWER, *Medieval People* (Penguin Books): c. IV.

14. THE ENGLAND OF THE CANTERBURY TALES AND PASTON LETTERS

Introductory

D. TAYLOR, *Chaucer's England* (Dobson).

Authorities

G. M. TREVELYAN, *English Social History* (Longmans): cc. I–III.

G. G. COULTON, *Chaucer and His England* (Methuen's University Paperbacks).

POWER, op. cit.: c. III.

APPENDIX IV

Sketch-maps Illustrating the Growth of Britain

H

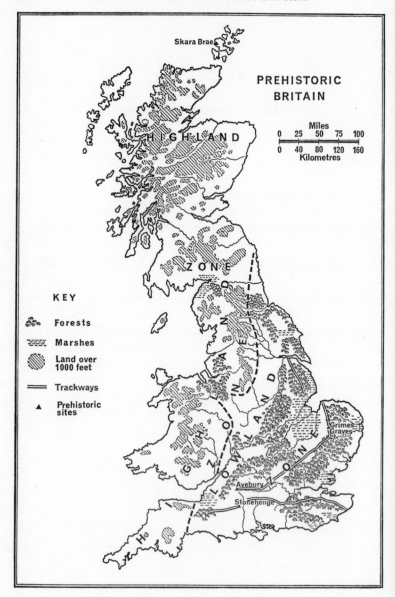

Skara Brae

PREHISTORIC
BRITAIN

Miles
0   25   50   75   100
0   40   80   120   160
Kilometres

H I G H L A N D

Z O N E

KEY

Forests

Marshes

Land over
1000 feet

Trackways

▲ Prehistoric
   sites

Grimes
Graves

Avebury

Stonehenge

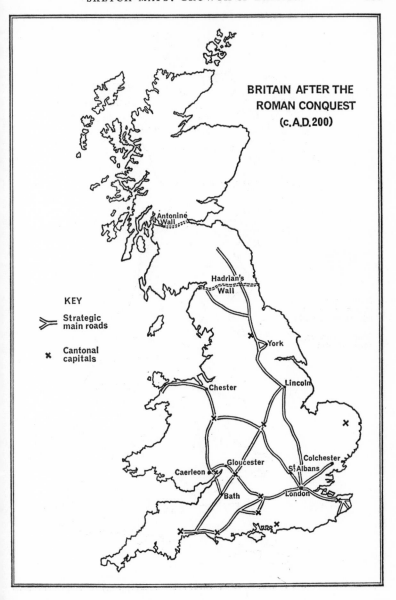

BRITAIN AFTER THE
ROMAN CONQUEST
(c. A.D. 200)

Antonine
Wall

Hadrian's
Wall

KEY

Strategic
main roads

Cantonal
capitals

York

Chester

Lincoln

Caerleon

Gloucester

Colchester

St Albans

Bath

London

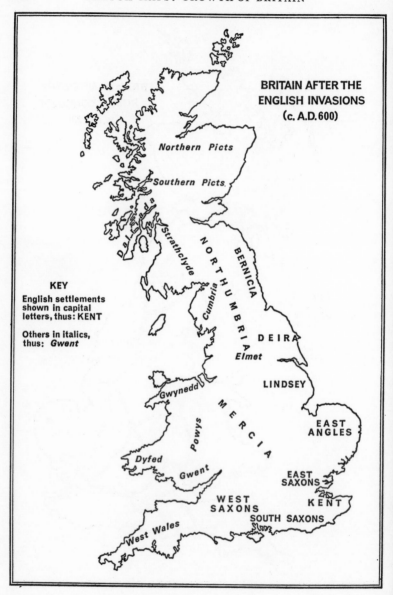

BRITAIN AFTER THE
ENGLISH INVASIONS
(c. A.D. 600)

Northern Picts

Southern Picts

Dalriada

Strathclyde

NORTHUMBRIA

BERNICIA

Cumbria

KEY
English settlements
shown in capital
letters, thus: KENT

Others in italics,
thus: *Gwent*

DEIRA

Elmet

LINDSEY

Gwynedd

M E R C I A

EAST
ANGLES

Powys

Dyfed

Gwent

EAST
SAXONS

WEST
SAXONS

KENT

SOUTH SAXONS

West Wales

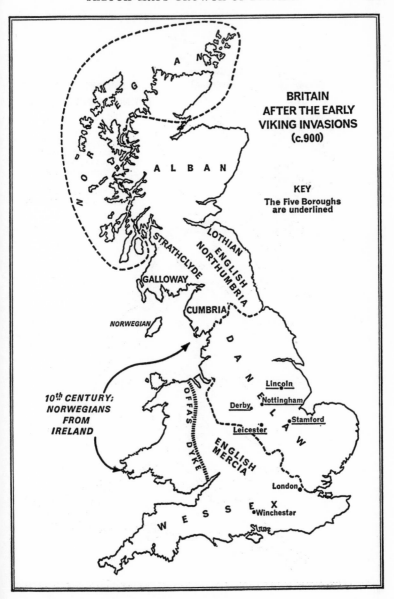

BRITAIN
AFTER THE EARLY
VIKING INVASIONS
(c.900)

KEY
The Five Boroughs
are underlined

N O R W E G I A N

A L B A N

STRATHCLYDE

GALLOWAY

LOTHIAN

ENGLISH
NORTHUMBRIA

CUMBRIA

NORWEGIAN

D A N E

L A W

OFFA'S DYKE

10th CENTURY:
NORWEGIANS
FROM
IRELAND

Lincoln

Derby   Nottingham

Stamford

Leicester

ENGLISH
MERCIA

London

W E S S E X

Winchester

**BRITAIN AFTER
THE NORMAN CONQUEST
(c.A.D.1100)**

KEY
Towns of special importance
are named, together with
the Cinque Ports
(which are underlined)

Arrows show lines of advance
of Marcher Lords into Wales

NORWEGIAN

SCOTLAND

Edinburgh

ENGLAND

BISHOPRIC
OF DURHAM

NORWEGIAN

York

EARLDOM
OF CHESTER

EARLDOM
OF
SHREWS-
BURY

WALES

Lincoln

Hereford

Norwich

Gloucester

Oxford

London

Bristol

Canterbury

Sandwich
Dover
Hythe
Romney
Hastings

Winchester

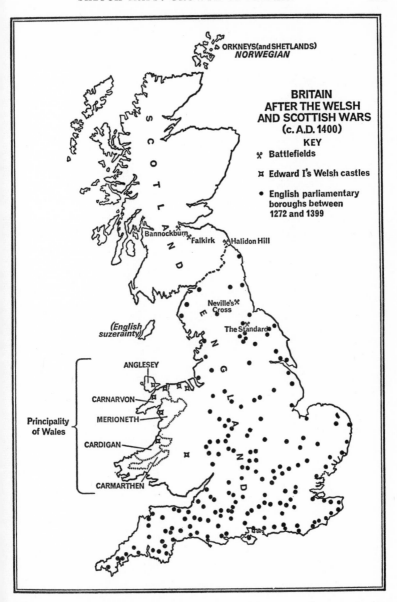

ORKNEYS(and SHETLANDS)
NORWEGIAN

**BRITAIN
AFTER THE WELSH
AND SCOTTISH WARS**
(c. A.D. 1400)
KEY

⚔ Battlefields

⌘ Edward I's Welsh castles

● English parliamentary
boroughs between
1272 and 1399

SCOTLAND

Bannockburn ⚔Falkirk ⚔Halidon Hill

Neville's ⚔
Cross

The Standard●

*(English
suzerainty)*

ENGLAND

ANGLESEY

CARNARVON

MERIONETH

**Principality
of Wales**

CARDIGAN

CARMARTHEN

INDEX

INDEX

Numbers in italics refer to Plates